The 7½ Habits of Highly Humorous People

David M. Jacobson, MSW, LCSW
Illustrations by Philip Rubinov-Jacobson

"The 7 ½ Habits of Highly Humorous People," by David M. Jacobson.
ISBN 978-1-60264-037-5.

Library of Congress Control Number: 2007931225.

Published 2007 by Virtualbookworm.com Publishing Inc., P.O. Box 9949, College
Station, TX 77842, US. ©2007, David M. Jacobson. All rights reserved. No part of this
publication may be reproduced, stored in a retrieval system, or transmitted in any form
or by any means, electronic, mechanical, recording or otherwise, without the prior
written permission of David M. Jacobson.

Manufactured in the United States of America.

Dedication:
To My Mother, Rose

The Lesson

So long ago
she gave me birth
and taught me how precious
a life is worth
through all these years
I've thought of her
and how special the lessons
she taught me were
Now it's New Years
time to reflect
and search my soul
with introspect
one result
of looking within
reveals the coaching
of my closest kin
the richest lesson
from her I find
was the value
of being kind

Acknowledgements:

I would like to thank David Lempert, my best friend, who has been encouraging me to write this book for the past twenty years. I would also like to thank my family, because they have to live with me and I have to live with them. My wife Laurie has been a great help with this book; her insights and comments have helped to shape it, even though she hasn't read it. My brothers, Alan, Mr. Genius IQ and scrabble master, and Philip, the great artist who honors me by permitting his work to be placed in this book in their black and white format, which does not do them justice, and my sister Jessica, the fun loving animated sister who is oversensitive and buys million dollar homes, but is poor. I mention these siblings because if I don't mention them and this becomes a best seller, I'll never hear the end of it. Such helpful comments as "Burn it, and try again" and "You want people to pay money for this?" But there were also comments like, "I laughed a lot" and "I like that it has meat in it, even though I'm a vegetarian." Other honorable mentions include Ginnie Genovese, Juliet Hunt and Kevin Purcell. I apologize for not mentioning your name, but I would also like to acknowledge you, the reader, because many readers don't read the acknowledgements. Statistics show that if you are mentioned in a book, you are more likely to like it and give positive feedback about it.

Table of Contents

Preface

What to do after you bought this book and found that you don't like it.

If you don't like the book, turn it into a positive experience anyway! Use your creative mind to come up with uses for it. Use it in the fireplace, emergency toilet paper, make paper airplanes out of the pages, cut out the middle and hide your drugs in it (I do mean prescription medications, of course). Give it as a gift to someone you don't like with a note that reads "You REALLY need this!" Give it to a kid to crayon in. Better yet, crayon all over it and then walk into your kid's room, mad as hell and ask, "Who crayoned in this book?"

Another ten reasons to buy this book:

1. You will not need a dictionary when you read it. (Unless you don't read/understand English).
2. It's a quick read that will put a smile on your face.
3. It's a fun conversation starter, just by holding it!
4. It is as educational as it is amusing.
5. It's filled with ideas to prompt you to think of humor in a new way.
6. There's not much repetition in it. There's not much repetition in it.
7. You will be better able to communicate with others after reading it.
8. It makes a great gift!
9. It will inspire you and raise your understanding of humor.
10. Okay, nine reasons.

Where to read this book: This book enjoys comfy couches and recliners, fluffy beds, and occasionally restaurants. It prefers to be seen in classy restaurants rather than fast food establishments though. There is a chance that just by reading this book in public you will attract many members of the opposite sex, that is unless you are gay or lesbian, bi-sexual or transgendered, in which case you may attract members of your own sex, others like you or both. Woody Allen said, "Bisexuality immediately doubles your chances for a date on Saturday night." This statement is statistically correct.

Some people just seem to be born naturally funny and with a great sense of humor. This does not mean though, that you cannot improve your sense of humor or humorous habits. At least, I hope it doesn't mean that because if it does then this whole book is a waste of your time and my chances of making a lot of money off of it will be seriously affected. Think about it. By the time you reach the last page of this book, you will be well on your way to becoming a Highly Humorous Person. Of course if you go straight to the last page, you could still be humorous, but you would more likely be a lazy humorous person and they just aren't as funny, because they're not willing to WORK on the humor. Yes, humor is a tough job, but someone's got to do it. If you're that someone in a group of people, you will be recognized as the greatest member of the group and people will probably come up to you and give you money or gifts.[1] These are the types of things that happen to people that read this book.

People define riches in various ways. If I am with another person and that person is suffering in some way, I consider myself richer if I am able to give them a smile or laugh, and relieve their suffering, especially while writing run on sentences at the same time. You too can be richer

---

[1] Disclaimer: This is not a promise and actual results will very.

for the experience of sharing your sense of humor and run-on sentences. A person is beautiful if they can share a rich sense of humor and love for their fellow beings. This is the type of thing you should be thinking or doing while being.

David Jacobson

Postface

"From the moment I picked your book up until I laid it down I was convulsed with laughter. Some day I intend reading it." Julius Henry (Groucho) Marx.

Postcard to my father-in-law from Groucho Marx[2]

Two comments from Howard Hughes: 1. *"This book will never fly."* 2. *"I'm still dead."*

Actual letter from Howard Hughes to my father-in-law[3]

---

[2] Available to the highest bidder when my wife is out of town.
[3] Also available to the highest bidder when my wife is out of town.

Fast Forward

The proper way to read a fast forward is at twice the normal speed of speech. Try to read out loud as fast as you can:

This fast forward was written by a person so famous, that he or she wouldn't allow their name to be mentioned in the book.

Rules for reading this book:

Rule One – Do not attempt to read this book in the dark. It's not good for your eyes and I can't believe I even have to give you this rule!

Rule Two – You must smile within reading every five pages or stop reading and return to the book later. Not smiling is a sign you're too tired to read and will not get as much out of the reading as when you are more alert; the only exception to this rule is if you can't sleep and are trying to put yourself to sleep, in which case you should go directly to the most boring pages in this book. No one really knows where they are though.

Rule Three – Don't take notes - this is not a test. Feel free to mark it up though. Underline clever phrases and parts that give you clairvoyant insights.

Rule Four –There are no rules. Whoever heard of laying out rules for properly reading a book anyway?

The fast forward you just read is an example of using humor to improve your communication, habit 5 of the 7 ½ habits of highly humorous people. I simply used my humorous imagination to pretend that an actual famous person wrote this instead of me. This makes me feel better and attempts to make the reading more enjoyable for you.

Backward

Most books have a forward, but instead this book has a backward. I thought that you, the highly humorous reader, who has a far greater sense of humor than most readers, would prefer a backward, not to mention a fast forward and the value added postface, all for the same "average priced book." No additional charges were incurred for these added values and no animals were harmed.

The only thing more fun than writing a humor book is reading one. Movies are also more fun. So is sleeping and sex, oh and listening to music, also about twelve other activities that come to mind. Actually, most things are more fun than writing a humor book.

You can buy someone something and call it a present, but humor is truly a greater gift.

In sharing my humor with you I am reminded of that famous Chinese proverb:

Give a man a fish, and you feed him for a day. Teach a man to fish, and you feed him for a lifetime.

I would add..."Give him a grill and he'll enjoy all that fish a lot more."

The fabric of humor.

Humor can be viewed like a quilt. Just like a quilt represents the many racial, nationality, religious, and cultural groups that are part of the American population, so the type of humor you use reflects your personal tastes, background and your socioeconomic, religious, pseudo scientific new age perspectives.

I hope you enjoy the tapestry of humor woven throughout this book.

Introduction

I spoke to my sister Jessica and asked her if she had read my book yet and she responded *"No, I was too depressed."*[4]

"My life has been one great big joke. A dance that's walked. A song that's spoke, I laugh so hard, I almost choke. When I think about myself." Maya Angelou[5]

Do you watch in puzzlement while everyone else in the room is laughing and think that you just don't get it? Do you often think, "That was so funny, I wish I had said that?" Well this book is for you. Are you the funniest person you know? Well this book is for you too. Are you a short Jewish arthritic social worker with a bald spot? Well, you may have written this book.

First, we need to talk, so please sit down and relax. Get comfortable; put that velvet Elvis pillow behind your head. Laugh when you think something your reading is funny. If you happen to be on a plane right now next to someone, just laugh out loud and say something like: "Wow, this is great!" Show them the book cover. This way I may get another book sale and you will get the satisfaction of knowing that you personally helped the author. When I finally become famous, you can say, "Yeah. I'm the one that helped that guy get to where he is today!"

---

[4] My sister is not really a depressed person. She is a vibrant and life-of-the-party type person, though the statement above is true.

[5] From *Masks* adapted by Maya Angelou from Paul Lawrence Dunbar's *We Wear the Mask*

Let's get one thing straight before we get any further into this book. This may be a highly humorous book written by a certified, authentically highly humorous person, but that does not mean that this book is frivolous, or without important content. This is not a "joke" book, although it will have many humorous moments. This is a 'fun' book full of substance and with an underlying serious message. HUMOR CAN CHANGE YOUR LIFE FOR THE BETTER. HUMOR CAN GET YOU THROUGH THE MOST CATASTROPHIC EVENTS OF YOUR LIFE. A HIGHLY HUMOUROUS PERSON IS THE MOST RESILIENT PERSON ON THE PLANET.

What if there wasn't any humor in the world? Think about that for a moment. What if humor didn't exist? Could you live without humor? Would you want to? We need laughter sustenance almost as much as we need other basic necessities.

I've experienced many hardships in my life including the loss of my father at age eight and a diagnosis of severe arthritis at age twenty-two. I lost physical abilities, lost a pain-free body, lost my self-confidence, lost my wallet, but that's a different story. Did humor make a difference in my life? Yes. I can't promise that humor can turn you into a strong, handsome, successful, intelligent, and modest person like myself, but I can promise that you will be better off for reading this and trying than doing nothing at all.

If I had to sum up what I would hope you walk away with after reading this book it would be the message of the following poem I wrote during an arthritis flare-up:

A Place for Pain

I open the door, pain walks in
Filling my home with darkness and discontent

I open the door, love walks in
Replenishing the bedroom
I open the door, faith walks in
Illuminating my living room
I open the door, hope walks in
Filling the kitchen with wonderful smells
I open the door, joy walks in
I explain that she has the wrong address
She should be next door
She comes in anyway
Joy, like pain
Knows not of manners or proper protocol
I open the door, humor walks in
It fills the empty spaces
Pain is still here
But it has little room.

All the positive emotions will reduce the power of pain and put it in its proper place, leaving it with less room to roam free and fill your life. Of all of these positive emotions, it is the power derived from a high sense of humor that has been my anchor, to hold me fast throughout the chaotic storms of life.

What is a highly humorous person and how will you know when you run into one?

First of all, if you are a highly humorous person and you run into a mirror, it will be obvious you are running into one. You will also recognize a highly humorous person because if you run into one, you will feel happy, you'll be drawn to the person. You'll want to spend time with the person. You will enjoy their company whether simply on a flight seated next to them, or listening to their humorous observations while sitting around a fire with your homeless friends. If you ever get stuck in an elevator for any length of time, pray that it is with a highly humorous person and that the person did not eat beans for lunch. You may ask: "What about the guy that puts a lampshade on his head at the office party?" No, he is not likely to be a highly humorous person and could even be an idiot. "But David," you say, "You have a lampshade on your head on the cover of this book, so are you an idiot?" Yes, I could be, there are many contradictions in life and humor. It's based on chances. There is always a certain percentage chance that even highly humorous people like me will on some occasion (designing a book cover) put a lampshade on their head. Let's not stray from the important message here. Don't think that a highly humorous person is not a highly skilled expert. It takes high cognitive abilities, quick wit and fine-tuned perceptive skills as well as creativity, a vivid imagination, insight, self-actualization, "people" skills and white teeth to be highly humorous. As you know most people are capable of possessing these traits; but without practice, vigilance, and a toothbrush, most will never reach their full potential of becoming a certified highly humorous person.

In order to understand what is meant by "habits of the highly humorous" we must first understand and agree on a proper *definition*. So what is a definition? According to The Winston Dictionary for Schools: Shorter Edition (1957), the definition of definition is: 1, the act of explanation; 2, an exact statement of the meaning of a word, term, phrase. Now that we agree on a proper definition, I will attempt to define "humor" and "habits" later in this book, after I've had a chance to recover from defining definition.

Overview of the 7 ½ Habits of Highly Humorous People. Are you an HHP?

In order to save paper and trees, from this point on I will be referring to highly humorous people as HHPs.

The Half Habit: Mastering your thoughts. This is a half habit because you don't need the whole habit in order for it to be effective. It is the most difficult habit to maintain. This is the habit of changing your thoughts. Mastering your thoughts is a constant struggle; if you master them half the time, you'll be doing twice a well! The thoughts you share with others can have a profound influence on them.

Habit One: Treat humor as a necessity, not a luxury. Make humor a priority in your life and some of the side effects will include improved physical health, improved attitude and improved mental heath.

Habit Two: Use self-effacing humor. Its power comes from letting others know that you know your weaknesses and are comfortable with them knowing that you know they know.

Habit Three: Keep your eyes open for humorous situations or create them with your imagination. Humor is associated with cognitive mastery and promotes divergent thinking, a characteristic of creativity. In order to become highly humorous, you must discover or create unique associations among ideas. Children do this naturally. Adults who are able to retain their childhood fantasy skills live more humorously than the rest.

Habit Four: Use the power of humor and its positive influence on yourself and others. There is a connection between sense of humor and overall well-being; your sense of humor may also help others to improve their well-being. Human being and well-being are not synonymous, could be an oxymoron, but not necessarily.

Habit Five: Use your humorous imagination to improve your communication. Humor is a great communication tool. Humor helps you to have fun, which reduces anxiety and knocks down common roadblocks that impede communication. The best form of communication is "Cohumorcation,"® which you'll learn more about later.

Habit Six: Humorize with humorgy. When you can take all parts of yourself and add the spirit of humor, you experience wholeness in a way that can't be described, only felt. Be open to that and you'll have humorgy. To "humorize" is to see humor in common situations where others don't. To humorize with humorgy is to have the ability to use humor to change your feelings and thoughts and the thoughts and feelings of others.

Habit Seven: Act like the highly humorous person you've become or are becoming. This means acting as if you are a highly humorous person. With this attitude, you'll be able to reinforce and strengthen the other habits.

Chapter One:
My theory of humor
An introduction to Humor Spirit Theory

"Analyzing humor is like dissecting a frog. Few people are interested and the frog dies of it." E.B. White

What is Humor Theory?

"Humor Theory is a field of study that describes the elements of humor and includes the development and application of methods for analyzing and composing humor. Broadly, theory may include any statement, belief, or conception of humor. A person who studies or practices humor theory is a humor theorist. Humor Theory generally attempts to reduce the practice of amusing and laughing into rules and ideas."[6]

Humor theorists have struggled over what makes something funny ever since there have been humor theorists. Modern humor theorists have been around for over a hundred years; whereas ancient humor theorist lived in ancient times. Some have discovered what variables make specific acts funny, but their explanation of why those same variables don't make all situations funny is lacking. According to my theory, the answer is simple. It is because we are all different and no two people can ever see the same situation with the same perception, although we can see the same situation with

---

[6] (Source: http://uncyclopedia.org/wiki/Humor_Theory)

kindred spirits and that bonds us by the connection between our spirits.

There are several theories of humor but most readers of this book are not interested in theory; however they do want to know how they can improve their sense of humor while having an enjoyable read. I will continue with a brief overview of theory and then straight into the meat, or for vegetarians - the protein substitute, of the book.

With this book, I am introducing a new theory. **Humor Spirit Theory.** Humor has a spiritual aspect derived from what some call our eternal soul that is often overlooked while being defined. Not only is there a higher power, there is a humor power. The basic premise is "humorgy." Humorgy is what I call the humor force. We know that humor is the quality that makes something laughable or amusing. Its definition is based on your unique personality and the life experiences that shape your perceptions. This is why what you find amusing may not be amusing at all to another individual with totally different life experiences and personality. Humorgy is intuition, insight on a sub-cellular inter-spiritual level (whatever that means) that comes from a place deep within your inner being. Many have thought of these concepts before, but never put them into words, or died suddenly just as they were about to tell someone else about it, or they used a different format to explain the same concepts. For whatever reasons, many of these concepts are universal; therefore most highly humorous people will recognize these concepts and say *"Hey, that's my idea."* I know I have said that while reading many others such as Dave Barry and some books by my colleagues in the National Speakers Association.

So what is humor? Every book ever written on this subject struggles to resolutely define what it is. I would like to say this one is an exception. I would like to say it, but it is a matter of fact that the definition depends on so many mitigating factors that there is no one proper definition that will please everyone. So if this one doesn't please you, I'm sorry, but you'll just have to live with it. Since we all perceive humor through our own senses, which clearly only belong to us, then it is fair to say there are billions of definitions of humor. For brevity's sake, I will use only one definition. A sense of humor is the result of the use of your ability to think and be amused by yourself, someone else, or a situation. Your sense of humor is judged by others, by your ability to share these thoughts and musings with them. Most people judge someone's sense of humor by some or all three of these characteristics: someone you can easily get to laugh and they laugh often, someone who laughs at the same things as you do, someone who creates humor seemingly without effort.

Humor is that state of being where one has an inner feeling of happiness brought on by observing or thinking about persons, places or things that amuse them. Humor is something that HHPs comprehend, express, create, appreciate and are drawn to. For a baby, humor is a funny face that makes them laugh; for an Einstein, humor is a disjunction of two concepts brought together in an unusual way that brings about a new view of the otherwise unrelated topics or issues that is amusing. This reveals her[7] knowledge of the cosmic joke of the universe.

The planets revolve around the solar system; we humans revolve around the soular system. Not only is there a higher power, there is a humor power. Humor is also spelled humour and not often misspelled huemore. Fact: The origin of the term derives from the humeral medicine of the ancient Greeks, which stated that "*a mix of fluids known as humours controlled human health and*

---

[7] If you're male, substitute "his" for "her," if you're a male who wishes he was female, leave it alone.

emotion."[8] Apparently the ancient Greeks were right in thinking that "humours" influenced health and emotions.

Humor Spirit Theory is based on understanding humorgy. Humorgy as mentioned describes the humor force or laughing force. Sometimes you may intuitively know what will bring a smile to another's face. That is humorgy. Ruach is Hebrew for 'breath,' and literally means spirit. The root of the word is related the meaning of wind. This is why "breaking wind" is amusing, because it is so closely related to humorgy. Want to hear something funny? Listen to some types of wind. Not all wind is funny, but passing gas generally is. Sometimes loud ones are funny, but also the quieter poppers can be quite amusing as well. Resorting to this kind of humor (often referred to as toilet humor) is sometimes considered a desperate attempt at being funny when someone is not sophisticated enough to get a chuckle with clean humor. As you see, I am not below resorting to this type of humor in book format, although you are not likely to hear me use it as a professional speaker on the platform and as a professional member of NSA.[9]

Do you use the lightness of humor to diffuse anger? Your sense of humor is like a muscle; the less you use it the weaker it gets, the more you use it the stronger it gets. Repeat this positive self-talk statement to yourself: *"By exercising my sense of humor it grows stronger like marble-... cake."*

If you expect the best, but experience the worse, you can still make the best of the worse experience; the opposite is also true.

---

[8] http://www.internetencyclopedia.org/index.php/Humour
[9] NSA is the National Speakers Association
http://www.nsaspeaker.org/speaker_detail/20034.shtml

Humor tastes sweet, but ridicule tastes bitter. Humor is a great way to show gratitude. Gratitude is just an attitude with a grrr in front of it.

The Ruach is also associated with the lungs, with the breath, and the element of air. Just as we breathe life into another with mouth-to-mouth resuscitation, so humor breathes energy into your spirit. Laughter also involves the lungs; without lungs you can't laugh. Come to think of it, without lungs you can't do much of anything. The result of regular laughter is a healthier person and the ability to improve your health more quickly. This is humorgy. Hopefully, you will find something useful in the concept of humorgy.

Humorgy is more than a thought process, more than a physiological reaction, more than a "mind trick" and more than a response to any of your senses such as sight or sound. You've heard of the *spirit of alcohol*. Most of you know when you are under the influence of the spirit of alcohol. Many have experienced *team spirit*. We've watched and participated in the *spirit of dance*. A very popular spirit is the spirit of belief. Many claim to have been *moved by the spirit*. Others claim to have been moved by National Van Lines, Inc.®

There is also a spirit of humor. We have all felt the spirit of humor. Sometimes it seems to just come upon you and you laugh. Sometimes you share a spontaneous humorous moment with another. You've looked into each other's eyes and both started laughing. You felt the connection. You are jointly experiencing the spirit of humor at that moment. There is truth in this statement whether you have a personal belief system or not. It has nothing to do with religion. It is universally human. It has everything to do with an unexplainable feeling that causes you to experience joy in the moment.

I recall one time I was overtaken by the spirit of humor during a serious lecture in a Yeshiva[10] in Jerusalem. I was sitting with a friend across from me and the Rabbi said something that wasn't particularly funny. What was funny was the look on my friend's face of total confusion and not understanding a word the Rabbi was talking about. I started laughing and then so did he. We were laughing hard enough that we had to bury our heads in our arms on the table. The fatal mistake we made, which gave the Humor Spirit total control of us, was that as we were regaining control, we both peeked up at each other at the same time. Seeing his eyebrow and one eye appear above his buried face beneath his arm and elbow was too much and I started cracking up, much louder than him. Then he became even louder when he looked under the table where I pointed and he noticed that I had totally pissed my pants. We were laughing so hard we had to get up and leave the room. As I left, still laughing quite loudly, my soaked pants were revealed to all and the spirit of humor spread throughout the room. Fortunately, the Rabbi also had a sense of humor and ended the lecture early, also laughing and explaining that sometimes we come closer to the almighty through laugher "as David apparently has done today." I believe the almighty was pleased, because as I left the building a heavy rain began, blessing and soaking me and hiding the evidence of my laughter-torn bladder so it would not be revealed to the public at large.

In Star Wars®, Obi-Wan Kenobi (Ben) said: "Well, the Force is what gives a Jedi his power. It's an energy field created by all living things. It surrounds us and penetrates us. It binds the galaxy together."

A basic premise was that the Force that existed could be tapped into by Jedi knights, evil Siths and just about

---

[10] A Yeshiva is either a Jewish rabbinic academy of higher learning or a delicatessen, I can't remember which.

anyone else in tune with it. There is also a laughing force (humorgy). Comedians and humorists have, to a certain extent, learned to master the humor spirit force.

Obi-Wan KeDavid: "The humor spirit force is an energy field created by all humorous things and things perceived to be humorous. It surrounds us and attempts to penetrate us, (*but not like an alien probe would*). It binds us with others so we see our connections. It can sometimes make people laugh, but it can also give someone an inner smile, a feel-good sensation that was inspired by another human being, creature, event, place, movie, book, etc." I have tested this belief many times and have found that the humor spirit force can be used to lighten someone's mood when they are anxious, angry, depressed, bored or just in a negative space. A master of humorgy (the humor force) is rare, but when you meet one, you will never forget it.

Humorgy is very attractive; even someone who may not be considered physically attractive will be seen as beautiful because of it. I mean, just look at what some of those Neanderthals and other cavemen looked like. It must have been humor that made them attractive, because paper bags weren't invented yet. It's their humorgy that made them attractive to one another.

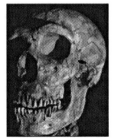

What Neanderthals looked like.

A Neanderthal using his sense of humor to get a date.

Take your spiritual self, your physical self, your mental self, your social self, your economic self, your political self, and your fish self or your self-fish.

When you can take all parts of yourself and add the spirit of humor you experience wholeness in a way that can't be described, only felt. Be open to that and you'll have humorgy. Humorgy is the absence of prejudice, judgment, and all negative aspects of life. It is an ideal that we can all strive to reach. When you master humorgy you can actually control, to a certain extent, the spirit of humor.

Chapter Two:
The ½ Habit
Changing negative thoughts to positive

Knock, knock!
"Who's there?"
Habit
"Habit Who?"
Habit we just get started with this chapter.

Wipe that Smile on Your Face
(to those that need help to laugh)

Wipe that smile off your face
Don't you know it's a disgrace
Do you think that that is funny
Upon my knee, I'll show you funny

This mindset has no room for humor
It grows and spreads just like a tumor
We must fight to change their thinking
Or they'll have us all a-stinking

Rules that restrict our free expression
Must be unlearned for a higher lesson
Laughter is our strongest weapon
To help them get to joyful steppin'

Help the people that are bitter
See the bright side, with a titter
Don't fear laughing in public places
It puts smiles upon others faces

So wipe that smile on your face
Do it with love and lots of grace

I'd like to introduce you to the half habit. "Half habit, this is a highly humorous reader. Highly humorous reader, this is a half habit." Shake hands, look at each other, and size each other up. Decide whether the half habit is attractive and whether the half habit has a hand. You may be wondering what a half habit is. A half habit is a habit that you don't need the whole of in order for it to be effective. It "enhances the flavor," as you'll discover later. This half habit is referring to inner thought. Throughout this book you've been talking to yourself. Hey, it's okay. Everyone does it. You may even be talking to yourself right now. "Gee, I'm talking to myself."

Don't let this quote about a common dark side thought you may have rule your life. "My life sucks." Rather, let this quote be a steady guide, "My life doesn't suck."

This is the half habit I refer to in the title and it is the habit of changing negative thoughts to positive ones. I have downgraded this habit to just one-half its strength because you don't need to do this one hundred percent of the time for it to be effective. Also because the title "The 8 Habits of Highly Humorous People" just doesn't sound as good. This half habit also happens to be the hardest to break and quite a challenge. Our mind is very busy all the time. It's human nature to have negative thoughts and times when we feel down. It is impossible to have only positive thoughts all the time. Therefore if you master it half the time, you'll be doing great! If you are able to use humor to change just half of your negative thoughts you'll be ten times healthier. Below is an example:

Negative Thoughts

"Nobody likes me." Change to: *"I haven't met everyone yet, there's still hope."*

"My body looks gross." Change to: *"Compared to what I'll look like in forty years, I don't look too bad."*

"People think I'm boring." Change to: *"People who think I'm boring don't really know me, or do they?"*

"Most people are out to get me." Change to: *"Most people are out to get me drunk."*

Suggested exercise: Make up some of your own.

I would venture to guess that about 75% of your thoughts are negative. I base this on statistics. As we all know 75% of statistics are statistically relevant. The other 25% fall into the category of not statistically significant or "made up." The above statistic I just cited falls into the category of "made up." That doesn't mean it may not be true though. As you'll remember from your logic course, just because a stork flies over your house when your wife is nine months pregnant doesn't mean she won't go into labor or that you're the actual father. Logic would dictate though that if your wife invites you to appear on the Jerry Springer Show®, there is a good chance she has been unfaithful. If your best friend also appears on the show, he is likely to be the one she was unfaithful with. In addition, she plans to use the money she makes off the show to get a high priced lawyer to remove all your current assets from you. This scenario is related to the concept of fallacy, which we don't even want to mention let alone go into explanations about. So let's just get back to negative self-thoughts.

Here are some negative words that have strong emotions connected to them.

FEAR: "I'm **afraid** to appear on the Jerry Springer show."

HARDSHIP: "If my wife robs me of all my assets it will be a **hardship** to maintain my extravagant mistress."

DREAD: "When I think of my best friend walking onto the Jerry Springer show with my wife, I get that **dreadful** feeling in the pit of my stomach."

DISAPPOINTMENT: "I can't believe my mistress is only in it for the money."

FRUSTRATION: "Every time my wife finds my hidden Viagra bottle, she throws it out."

Self-talk statements like the ones above make us feel sad or angry and result is increased stress and tension.

Take a look at these self-talk statements of an HHP:

SILLY: "To think my wife cheats on me, just because she sometimes comes home at 6am and hasn't had sex with me in two years, is just silly."

ENJOYMENT: "Wow, reading this book is so enjoyable!

PLEASURE: "The kiss on the cheek I get every week in exchange for paying for my mistress's apartment is pure pleasure."

CHEERFUL: "I love eating at this restaurant; the waitress I consistently over-tip is always so cheerful."

AMUSEMENT: "That conversation on the bus after losing my house and my car to my wife was so amusing, I'm glad I started it and got so many people involved."

How would the first set of thoughts affect your attitude as compared to the second set?

Ten years to the week after psoriatic arthritis seized many of my joints and changed my self-image from "Wonderman" to "Whimperman," I entered a 115-mile bicycle race around the perimeter of Tucson, Arizona. On November 17, 1990, El Tour de Tucson, (an Arthritis Foundation fund-raising event at the time), began. I had no idea how far I could really go and if I could make it to the finish line. At the end of that day and 115 miles later, I crossed the finish line. In a ceremony that evening, I received the "Jim Elliott Award," named for a man with epilepsy who holds the record for bicycling the longest distance in twenty-four hours. This award is presented to a bicyclist normally viewed by society as someone unable to compete in a strenuous athletic event. In other words, this award goes to someone with a chronic illness, labeled as "disabled," and not considered the type of person able to compete against "normal, healthy," individuals. I won the award and Jim Elliot himself presented it to me. I also received a silver medal.[11] The children, teens and young adults with arthritis looked to me as their champion. I was a living example that they had a future, that they still could accomplish great goals and that arthritis was not the only thing that defined them or mattered in life. Hope, faith, love and joy were with me that day, but more than all that my humor spirit was with me and helped keep me going, as it still does to this day.

Aaron's Heart by Philip Rubinov-Jacobson

---

[11] It wasn't really made of silver.

After my bicycling event and the award ceremony, I received media attention due to my accomplishment. TV news, radio and newspapers all said how the following year, I would be going for the gold. The following year, on my first training ride, I called my wife Laurie to pick me up after going just one mile. My knees and back were shot and prevented me from even going one mile on the bike. My ego was involved. Here I was supposedly the inspirational example, the "Jim Elliot Award winner," the one who overcomes all obstacles. The one who would cross the next finish line with a gold medal and I couldn't even ride a mile. The optimistic, humor-powered David was feeling depressed. At this point, when our thoughts stress us out, we usually get very concrete. Either I go for the gold or I don't. I felt my only choice was to give up. This type of thinking is negative. Back to that half habit. I needed to use my humor spirit to come up with an alternative. Maybe I could use a fishing pole to hook another bike-rider and catch a free ride. Maybe I could buy a giant magnet and get pulled by another rider. As soon as the humor spirit takes over, you go into the creative mode. It was in this mode that I came up with a solution to saving face about not riding the bike again. The solution allowed me to feel good about not riding the bike in the next El Tour and also about remaining physically active. As I was brainstorming about hooking on to other riders and getting giant magnets to be pulled by them, this silly thought process led my humor spirit to suggesting I ride my unicycle instead. I actually do have a unicycle. In graduate school I used it to get around the huge ASU campus. I could barely walk 100 feet at the time, but I could unicycle long distances, keeping the weight off my partially fused and swollen ankles.

Now, ten years after graduation, I got back on it, kind of as a joke, but found a few miles later, I didn't have the pain in my back and knees that I had experienced on my bike. My back was straight and the range of motion in my knees was less stressful. With humorgy, you can trick yourself. My goal was to ride fifty miles on the unicycle in the El Tour de Tucson. The miles went by slowly and painfully. Fighting the cold, harsh wind in my face, almost blowing me off the unicycle, and barely having enough strength to stay on the unicycle, I continued. At forty-eight miles my body told me I was done. My humor spirit told me I wasn't. It said "Go a couple more miles and you can laugh about this and tell stories to your grandchildren for the rest of your life." I imagined myself with my grandson saying, "Did I ever tell you the story of how I rode fifty miles on a unicycle against a cold brisk wind?" "Yeah grandpa, only a hundred times!" That smile gave me the strength to continue a little further. I used humorgy to bolster my will. Knowing that the fundraiser was for the Arthritis Foundation and would benefit children with arthritis was another incentive. I also liked the idea of being an inspiration to these kids. The other "trick" was to call upon the spiritual strength of my own father. Upon reaching the point of finally quitting, I looked up to the sky and thought of my father and his iron will and prayed for some of that will and the strength to continue this journey. Suddenly the wind, which was almost blowing me over, stopped and it was just the reprieve I needed to continue on. It lasted just long enough for me to regain my strength and get my second wind. I tricked myself into riding a unicycle fifty miles in 6 hours and 59 minutes. Yes, you can trick yourself into accomplishing more than you could ever dream possible. To do this you must use the compelling combination of humor, positive thinking, tricking the mind, connecting to your will, connecting to what you perceive to be a greater spirit and connecting with the spirit of the creator.

Your will is another part of humorgy. Your will gives you the ability to stretch yourself just a little beyond what you believe to be your limits. Humor can help strengthen your will through the half habit of positive self-talk. One of the reasons I was able to complete my fifty mile unicycle ride was due to spiritual strength. Humor plays a part in spiritual strength, so does my father and the religion of my fathers, which has given me the feeling of standing on the heads of giants. These giants don't particularly like having their heads stood on, but they understand why their heads are being stood on. We all have countless generations of spiritual tradition that came before us and support us in times of adversity. This is the kind of help that can't be measured scientifically but still plays a part in completing any task that may seem insurmountable or unobtainable.

Painting of Israel Jacobson by Philip Rubinov-Jacobson

My father was a master of humorgy. When he entered a room it never went unnoticed. Humorgy is related to charisma, another word hard to define, but understood. We know what we mean when we say, "That guy has got charisma!" The common element between charisma and humor is magnetism. People are attracted to the humorous/charismatic personality.

What do positive humor spirit thoughts say to you? "Don't pass gas loudly enough to be heard." "If you sneeze, make sure no boogers are stuck on you." "Don't walk around with poop on your pants." "Don't talk to a large audience with your fly opened," etc. [12] What prompts your negative thoughts? When you watch too much negative news or read the paper and focus on the negative stories, do you start to worry and become afraid? Have you ever looked at newspaper headlines and tried to see how funny they can be by reframing the meaning?

Here are some common examples you are likely to have already seen:

- Police Begin Campaign To Run Down Jaywalkers
- Farmer Bill Dies In House
- Is There A Ring Of Debris Around Uranus?
- Prostitutes Appeal To Pope
- Panda Mating Fails: Veterinarian Takes Over
- Enraged Cow Injures Farmer with Ax

If you look for these types of slips of the tongue, unintentionally suggestive and grammatical errors, you're bound to come up with some funny headlines once in a while.

What would happen if you skipped some of your negative thought provoking habits a few times a day? How many more positive thoughts would you have

---

[12] I have done all these things.

because of this minor change? Do you experience any repetitive thoughts that occur over and over? Do you experience any repetitive thoughts that occur over and over?[13] Do you experience any repetitive thoughts that occur over and over? "What's my financial situation today? I better worry about money again, because I haven't worried about my financial situation since yesterday!" If you have money worries, I suggest you read Dave Barry's "Money Secrets." I must comment that his dedication in the book is very similar to what my original dedication was going to be for this book. I have friends and family that can verify this. My point is that the humor spirit causes many humorists to come up with very similar and sometimes the same ideas, independently. Often we feel others are "stealing" our ideas. This of course is true. People are often stealing our ideas. Other times though, people just come up with the same ideas independently, because they have tapped into a universal source.[14] What gives you positive thoughts? Comedy Central? A nice song? A book by your favorite comedian? This book? Old Willie Kanute who lives down the street and always has something outrageous to say? The best way to influence your negative thoughts is to become more aware of what initiates them as well as what initiates your positive thoughts.

Use the hammer of humorous habits to beat negative thoughts into submission. Warning: the following thought processes may be hazardous to your humor and health.

The following cognitive distortions are easy traps to fall into.[15]

---

[13] Reason #6 to buy this book on page 5, may not be true.

[14] The tiny, green, floating alien, "The Great Gazoo" of the Flintstones.

[15] Burns, David D., MD. 1989. The Feeling Good Handbook. New York: William Morrow and Company, Inc.

All-or-Nothing Thinking: Either I ride the entire 115 mile El Tour or it doesn't mean anything.
Counterattack – The creative solution of unicycling instead.

Overgeneralization: Because I couldn't ride the whole El Tour, I'll never be able to do anything physically demanding again.
Counterattack – Not true, I'm overgeneralizing.
Stereotyping also falls into this category. All lawyers are unethical, all politicians lie.[16]

Mental Filter: Hearing that I'm a valued employee goes through the mental filter as – She's just saying that to make me feel better, she doesn't really believe that.
Counterattack – How do I know she doesn't believe that? Why do I negatively filter interpretations into a bad outcome?

Filtering: Putting a giant spotlight on one negative occurrence and using it to broadly explain an entire day. "Waking up late will ruin my whole day."
How come we never spotlight one good thing that happens and then think, "Wow, my whole day will be amazing because I woke up early?" Filtering blinds us to everything else, but one small aspect of what we're looking at.

Disqualifying the Positive: When complimented, I can think, "Oh, he just said that because he feels bad that I have arthritis. He doesn't mean that."
Counterattack: Again it's refusing to see anything positive, just the negative.

---

[16] Okay, that one happens to be true.

Choices: Upon your 90th birthday, please choose one of the following statements that best fits your life:

Choice One: "In my life, I spent most of my time worrying about things that might have happened, but didn't, or happened, but I couldn't change."

Choice Two: "In my life, I spent more time using my sense of humor than thinking negative worrying thoughts."

Chapter Three:
Habit One
Treat humor as a necessity not a luxury

We need to eat, sleep and use the bathroom. At least I do. I mean, if you're got the runs and really have to go to the bathroom urgently, you don't say "Ah, maybe I'll use the bathroom;" no, you run to it! Treat your humor that importantly and your sense of humor will greatly improve. If you treat humor as urgently as your physical needs, you'll be well on your way to being an HHP. We need to smile and laugh and see humor every day, every chance we get. On a first date is humor a luxury or necessity? If you want a second date, humor better be part of that first date.

There are times not to laugh – not many though – like when telling someone very bad news or when someone is changing a flat tire, but other than that… There's usually a health benefit to laughter. A professional comedian is constantly looking for new material through their everyday interactions. Do you try to see the humor in all your interactions like a professional comedian would? If you seek out humor, it will find you. I am not a professional comedian, I am a humorist. A humorous person can also be a humorist. Most comedians are experts at stand-up comedy. Most humorists can make a point with humor. When you learn something in a humorous fashion, your chances of retaining the information are better, because you learned this new information in a fun way. It is common knowledge now that those who incorporate humor into educational material will have that material remembered by their pupils much longer than those that offer educational material in a drab, stuffy, cold or monotone way.

This first habit advises you to acknowledge the importance of appreciating humor. It's not how many jokes you can tell, it's how much you can appreciate a good one. How much you can appreciate the humor that surrounds you.

When my father died, my third grade class all made sympathy cards for me. When I came home from school my whole family was there and I began to read the cards. One of the cards said "Don't be sad, I would be sad too if my fat dad died." The word "fat" was crossed out. My uncle said, "Her dad probably saw her card and crossed the word 'fat' out." We all laughed. It was the first laugh we had had together since his death. It was a healing laugh and very cathartic. Humor allowed us to vent our welled up emotions. My father had a great sense of humor and all his children were blessed to inherit it.

Treating humor as a necessity, not a luxury, means treating your humor like a professional would treat their career. An HHP has passion, drive, and enthusiasm. These are things that this book cannot give you. They are internal mechanisms that can be further developed and improved upon if the desire to do so is strong enough. If you practice these new habits, you'll be on your way to further developing these internal mechanisms.

Parts of the humorgy whole:

Some of the parts of the humorgy whole are inherited traits, personal experiences and the influence of your environment. Also chicken wings, but they don't play a very big part. Though a humor gene has not yet been discovered, I am willing to bet that there is something in our DNA that helps to shape our sense of humor. Our experiences also have an influence. My parents had a great sense of humor, although my mother has tendencies toward sarcasm, which can be positive or negative, depending on its use. Where and how you grow up and live also has an impact. If you were raised in a home where at dinner you could joke and laugh and make mashed potato balls out of the mashed potatoes, like at my house, you are more likely to be more comfortable with using humor at the dinner table. If you were raised in a home where dinner was a sacred time of grace and gratitude, then you may have a little more difficulty being comfortable sharing humor over dinner. One isn't right and one isn't wrong, it simply represents different life experiences.

Two more parts of humorgy are imagination and fantasy. These provide us with the ability to create in our mind, actions, scenes and stories that don't exist in what we call reality.

A childhood memory:

At the age of five, my brother hid a surprise at the front door for me. I heard a knock at the front door of my house. "Go get the door, Day[17]," my ten-year-old brother Philip said to me. I walked over to the door and reached way up to the knob, turned it and opened the door.

There standing one foot tall at the door was a gnome, with a red hat hood, blue tunic and blue pointed slippers. Phil said, "Wow, It's the King of the Elves. You have to name him." "What are you gonna call him Day?" Asked my 7 ½- year-old sister. "His name is Chuckles." I answered without hesitation. Thus one of the first original creative namings I had done in my young life was a humor-related name. I was already treating humor with the importance it deserved. I believed "Chuckles" was

---

[17] Day was my nickname, short for David

alive. I had a very vivid imagination and swore I'd seen him move from the corner of my eye many times. His smile was magical and I thought he had magical powers!

My imagination kept me company wherever I went. I was never bored. As a child no one ever heard me say, "I'm bored." If you have an imagination, there is no excuse for claiming boredom. I could sit for hours watching people, thinking for example "… hmm that guy is a spy working for an enemy government and he's waiting to meet his contact."

As human beings, we are responsible for our own lives. An HHP is someone who has the strength to accept things that they can't change and change the things that are within their realm to change, for example, their underwear. A person with a poorly developed sense of humor is a person who is driven by feelings, circumstances, conditions, and the environment. They are tossed like a boat in stormy water without oars. An HHP is a person who is guided by his or her own purpose in life, with a clear mind, tempered with humor. A person with humorgy takes the bull by the horns and hangs wind chimes on them.

Events and Reactions:

We can't control the events that occur in our life but we can control our responses to those events. If you haven't heard this a hundred times already you haven't heard enough speakers or read enough self-help books. When conflicts and problems occur, they are usually the result of one of three situational areas: Our actions (the behavioral results of our attitude and underlying beliefs), the actions of others (the behavior of others, which results from their attitudes and underlying beliefs), or our memories of past actions or thoughts about future actions and situations.

Using our habits to change the way we influence ourselves and others is within the realm of our humor spirits influence. Those that treat their humor as a necessarily important component of their life evaluate their own behavior, find the humor in their actions, laugh at it and, as Paul Riser has said, "use humor to confront their problems not avoid them." The need for revenge and other petty useless actions dissolves. Humor brings wisdom to some, joy to others and smiles of amusement to just about everyone else.

Victor Frankl, a psychologist in the Freudian tradition, recognized that "between stimulus and response, man has the freedom to choose." The capacity human beings have of taking an objective stance toward their own life, or stepping outside themselves, is the basis, Frankl tells us, for humor. And, as he noted in the concentration camps, "Humor was another of the soul's weapons in the fight for self-preservation." [18]

As you see below, you decide the outcomes based on your responses to events.

Events and our Reponses: Which reaction do you think is better?

Event: Snide remark about weight: "When are you planning to go on a diet?

Reaction with humor: "When I start a new weigh of life."

Reaction without humor: "You son of a..." (you're so mad you pick up a refrigerator and throw it at the person, killing them instantly. You are convicted of murder and spend the rest of your life in prison.)

---

[18] Frankl, Viktor E., 1959. Man's Search For Meaning. Boston: Beacon Press

Event: Another snide remark: "Gee, you boomers think you are so special. Get over the sixties already and join the twenty-first century."

Reaction with humor: "Oh yeah." or "Youth cannot know how age thinks and feels. But old men are guilty if they forget what it is to be young."

Reaction without humor: The blood rushes to your head, you pop a vein in your temple and have a stroke. You spend the rest of your life drooling and can only enjoy such novels as <u>Fun with Dick and Jane</u> and <u>My Dog Spot</u>.

Event: You get pulled over for speeding, and when you roll down your window the cop says, "I've been waiting for you all day."

Reaction with humor: You respond, "Yeah, well I got here as fast as I could." When the cop finally stops laughing, he sends you on your way without a ticket.

Reaction without humor: You yell: "The driver you just let go by was driving ten miles per hour faster than me, if you did your job right, you would have pulled over the right guy!" The officer orders you out of the car. Tells you he suspects you're hiding drugs and does a cavity search.

We can't control the behavior of others, but we can control our response to those behaviors.

Several years ago I was invited to give a guest sermon at a Universalist Unitarian Church on the subject of "Humor and Spirituality." The church was on the other side of the city and I was already running a little behind. I jumped in the car and was on my way. I was getting stressed out watching the time. As I was rushing along in my lane, a guy cut into my lane right in front of me and his back bumper barely missed my front bumper by 1/16th of an inch, two atoms and one electron. We were heading for the light and I was pissed off! I couldn't wait to catch up to him and pull up next to him at the light so I could give him "the look." You know, "the look," that angry expression that tells someone "Gee, you are such an a-hole." It's kind of the equivalent of giving the finger, except with a facial expression instead. As I was pulling up, I thought about where I was going and for what purpose. I decided a different approach would be more in-line with my sermon and purpose in life. When we reached the light, the guy that cut me off turned to see my face. Just as I was reaching the light, I put my disabled placard on the mirror, pulled my arms out of my sleeves, tucked them in my shirt and bit the steering wheel with my teeth! He turned toward me at the light and saw a man with no arms, biting the steering wheel with his teeth. I slightly turned toward him, grinned at him with my teeth still holding the steering wheel and nodded my head. He had a shocked look on his face and appeared to feel awful for cutting off the poor pathetic armless guy. I was happy, he felt guilty, and this really defused the anger. I wasn't mad anymore and he wasn't either. Because humor was a necessity rather than a luxury at that moment, a potentially explosive situation turned into a milder humorous situation that was totally non-threatening. When my teeth hit that wheel, I was treating humor as a necessity.[19] [20]

---

[19] Apology to those with no arms: If you have no arms and were offended by this story, I am sorry, and don't have a leg to stand on. Please use your humorgy to forgive me.

[20] Apology #2: If you don't have a leg to stand on and were offended by the above statement, I am sorry about that too. Please use your humorgy to forgive me.

From this time forth, whenever you hear laughter, ask yourself, "Why did they laugh"? This question will improve your HHP skills and help you get a better idea of how humor works.

Chapter Four:
Habit Two
Use self-effacing humor

Know your weaknesses and turn them into strengths. Using self-effacing humor is the safest way to introduce humor to those you don't know that well. It helps build rapport and trust. Poke a little fun at yourself to open some communication. I can poke fun of my short-comings, because I happen to be short. You are always safe when you make yourself the "butt" of the joke, but never joke about the butt of someone else.

My wife came home after her complete physical when she turned forty. She was standing in front of the mirror in her underwear admiring herself. I came home not in the best mood, sore from my arthritis. I saw her and asked her, "What are you doing?" She said: "Dr. Wristen just gave me a physical and said I should be very proud of the shape I'm in. I have four children yet I have the physiology of a twenty-year-old." I responded: "Did she mention your forty-year-old ass?" Laurie gave me a look, thought for a second and said "No, your name didn't come up at all."[21] That response was the epitome of taking a potentially volatile situation and defusing the conflict with humor.

Become a master at self-effacing humor. Laughing at yourself is the highest and healthiest form of humor. Those that poke fun at themselves are giving the message:

---

[21] Okay, Laurie will tell you that this story isn't true, but I love this story.

"Hey, I know I'm _____ (fill in the blank), but I am still a person and I enjoy life."

I come from Rochester, New York, where having a nasal twang is normal. People from other parts of the country can tell I have a distinct accent. People that use self-effacing humor are more aware of these quirks because others know they won't get defensive if they mention them.

My version of self-effacing humor?

I'm a short slightly overweight Jewish arthritic middle-aged man with thinning scalp spots and graying streaks in his hair. If that's not funny, what is? Why can I poke fun at what I am today without jeopardizing my self-esteem? The memories of myself as that Olympian built "David" of yesteryear. That will sustain me the rest of my life and I am thankful for those memories. I'm sure you have memories that can sustain you too. It comes down to what is really important. Ego? Memory? Relationships? Clearly relationships are what drive me forward. It's exciting to have fun with new people and old people and even middle-aged boomers like myself. It never ends; we laugh until the day we die. The day we lose the ability to laugh at ourselves is the day we begin to die.

Be comfortable with your behind or any other part of you. I do not take my rear end very seriously and you shouldn't take my rear end seriously either. Chances are you may never have even seen my rear end so it would be difficult for you to take it seriously anyway. The more you look at your rear, the more you should be able to realize that it doesn't change based on how often you look at it, or feel about its current shape. If it currently looks great, that's great! Just keep in mind that eventually, if you live long enough, it will turn into Jell-O. ®

Self-effacing / self-deprecating humor works very well because it's really safe and does not lead to a loss of respect.

Self-effacing humor gets its strength from stressing your weaknesses. People that have the ability to laugh at themselves in just the right measure are perceived as secure, confident, strong, attractive and likeable.

Ray Romano is an expert at self-effacing humor and many other types as well. This could be because we both were born in New York and have the same birthdate: December 21, 1957. He's tall though, and Italian, whereas I only look tall[22] and Italian.

The fact that they let me in a movie with Gene Hackman has left me with no faith in show business.

Ray Romano

I'm confident in my self-deprecating humor. I am coming from a place of confidence. I KNOW I am an HHP and that feels good. It gives me that feeling of superiority that we all need to sustain us, but will never acknowledge in public that it is needed. I don't envy people. There's not enough time for envy or greed, or other negative thoughts.

Rodney Dangerfield is a great example of self-deprecating humor, but just look at the guy. He's ugly, stupid and fat.[23] I don't think he's really stupid. He knew if he had to go through life like that, it would be better to do it as a celebrity comedian than as some big fat dumb guy, as his life path could easily have taken.

---

[22] To toddlers
[23] This is known as a put-down, a type of inappropriate humor.

I was making love to this girl and she started crying. I said, "Are you going to hate yourself in the morning?" She said. "No. I hate myself now."
Rodney Dangerfield

Other examples:

I was so ugly when I was born, the doctor slapped my mother.
Henny Youngman

My one regret in life is that I am not someone else.
Woody Allen

You know you're old when someone compliments you on your alligator shoes and you're barefoot.
Phyllis Diller

Self-effacing humor gives others the message: I'm a human being just like you. I'm a human doing – doing things just like you. I'm a human saying, talking just like you and I'm a human listening – listening halfheartedly just like you.

We are not perfect. There are many imperfections you have that you can tease yourself about. How do you look walk, talk, sing, dance, drive, etc.? You could poke fun at yourself about any of those things. We just don't call them for what they are often enough. The person who is not afraid to use self-effacing humor will win the hearts and minds of all they meet in their everyday interactions. Take your imperfections less seriously and more like an HHP would.

If you have a fragile self-image, there are others types of self-effacing humor you should focus on. There is indirect self-effacing humor about your family, your neighborhood, your school, your team, etc. If your self-esteem were compromised, I would advise this type of humor. It still focuses on you rather than "them" but doesn't attack you personally.

Look for opportunities to see your humorous side and poke fun at it. This will be one of your most powerful tools to connect with others and a subtle way to show your strength.

Lincoln was a master of self-effacing humor. He viewed humor as a necessity to deal with his seemingly insurmountable troubles. He once said: "If this is coffee, please bring me some tea. If this is tea, please bring me some coffee." One of Lincoln's most famous quotes comes from addressing his cabinet with the following: "Gentlemen, why don't you laugh? With the fearful strain that is upon me night and day, if I did not laugh occasionally I should die, and you need this medicine as much as I do."[24]

Lincoln was a master storyteller. He often used self-effacing humor, he focused on his awkward gait, his being referred to as an uneducated rail-splitter and his not very photo-friendly face, using these characteristics to make himself the butt of his own jokes. His self-deprecating humor was very disarming to anyone who came into conflict with him.

What the Wounded Soldiers Thought:

Lincoln often visited hospitals in the Washington area. He would ask wounded soldiers about their health and would then entertain the patients with his stories. There is an unsubstantiated story that after one such visit, a journalist followed him to the same hospital and heard wounded soldiers laughing and talking about the

---

[24]http://www.mrlincolnandfriends.org Humor and Personality section.

President. The soldiers seemed in such good spirits that the journalist was curious, and overheard the soldier say that even though he lost a leg, he'd be glad to lose the other if he could hear more of the president's stories. Do you use your humor to inspire others? Does it inspire you to make the world a better place?

A master of self-effacing humor is confident and likeable. Self-effacing humor reveals the face of your inner humor self.

Chapter Five:
Habit Three
Keep your eyes open for humorous situations or create them with your imagination

Look at the context, and then change the context, accent, mannerism, voice, movement, expressions and actions to infuse humor into it.

Truck stuck under bridge.

How would you resolve this? [25]

---

[25] A child resolved the problem by telling adults to let the air out of the tires.

Therapeutic humor (To a sense of humor)

A poem that's funny and makes you smile
Can reduce your stress at least for a while

If you laugh hard enough to lose bladder control
You'll have a joyful and healthy soul (and wet pants)

So look for the humor in all that you do
And you'll see the world better with an outlook that's new

Just like in habit one where it's how much you appreciate humor rather than how many jokes you tell, the same is true for searching for humor. It is important to use your sense of humor in order to develop it to a higher level. The more you use it, the better your sense of humor will become.

Use your imagination, your observations and your fantasies to create humorous situations. The perfect example of creating humorous situations with his mind is the James Thurber character, Walter Mitty. If you haven't read the short story or seen the movie starring Danny Kaye, I highly recommend you do. In fact, I recommend anything written by James Thurber as he was a great American humorist.

I recall a time when I needed to create a humorous situation while working as a trauma social worker at UMC. The hospital setting can become very stressful, especially when you're telling loved ones that their spouse, mother, father, sister or brother did not survive. It was on a day like this when I was very busy and stressed out that I got on the elevator and it was empty. This rarely happens with the hustle and bustle of the hospital. I noticed I was the only one in, so I celebrated! I started jumping up and down and dancing, singing out loud, "Hurray, the elevator is empty!" When the doors opened, I walked out with a big smile on my face and truly feeling the spirit of humor. When I walked into the next patient's room, I was feeling happy – not a phony smile, but authentically happy. Do you think this can impact a patient? How many people walk into a patient's room truly happy? It's usually a relative or friend visiting that feels sad that they're there. Or it's a staff member who needs to get something from them, like blood, a stool sample, or urine. If you can walk into the room of an ill person truly feeling happy and sharing that mood with them, it may help. I recall walking into a room on a young man just after an "elevator celebration." I walked in smiling. He said, "It's good to see a smiling face." I said to him "I notice you're not smiling." He said, "You're right, because I'm scared to death about this surgery today. Thanks for helping me forget about it for a moment." He was there for a serious heart operation and was told he may not survive. I asked him, "What would make you feel less scared? He answered, "To know right away that I survived the surgery." I thought for a second and said, "Tell you what, how about if I put a big sign on the wall in post-op so that when you wake up the first thing you see is this sign that says 'YOU ARE HERE'." He said he'd like that.

After the surgery he told me that he awoke groggy but remembered about the sign, so he quickly looked at the wall and saw it. He smiled. A genuine wonderful smile. It may have been a silly little thing, but he told me that he would never forget that little piece of humanity waiting for him on the post-op room wall for as long as he lived. The humor used in the hospital setting is usually the witty and playful type. Fun chitchat between staff and patients eases the embarrassment of losing any modesty. Staff members see patients at their most intimate times.

Patients come into the hospital, are stripped of their clothes and put into a hospital gown with their ass hanging out. They are told when to eat, what to eat, when they can have visitors and when visitors must leave. Humor is used on a daily basis. You may not see it, but there is more humor in a hospital setting than a comedy club! It's just a little subtler. A toddler walks up to me and throws her diaper at me, I respond "Oh, a gift, thank you so much!" I walked into the room of a patient with severe cerebral palsy, and he said, "Need a milkshake? I can really stir!" Another patient passes gas quite loudly and tells me his roommate is a ventriloquist. A ninety-year-old patient asked me if I could send a female social worker with large breasts instead, I came back two minutes later with cloth stuffed in my shirt and told him "this is the best I can do." I walked into a room and a seventy-five-year-old female cancer patient lifted her gown to show me the wound on her behind. I said, "I'm a social worker, not a doctor." She said, "Yeah, well at my age, I rarely get to show my ass to anyone, so I'm going show it to whoever is willing to look!"

In the ICU I've worked with hundreds of patients so the odds of me remembering any particular one is against me. I had one former patient I met in a shopping mall. He said, "Hey David, remember me?" I had a look of non-recognition on my face. He said "Okay," pulled his head back as if he was looking directing up to the ceiling, then put a finger in his mouth and pulled it as if it was a tube jerking and stretching his cheek. He began to make a gurgling sound. I said "Oh, yeah, you were in the ICU!" If humor is needed anywhere, it's in a hospital setting. Humor is another way of letting patients know you care about them.

If you know what amuses you, you will be better able to see things humorously. Who's your favorite comedian? If you could see things through the eyes of your favorite comedian, do you think you'd have a better outlook? If you know what amuses you and what types of humor are attractive to you, you'll have a better focus on what types of humor to look for, types of comedians to watch, types of humor books to read, etc. What styles do you like?

Types of humor and humor styles:

Observational Humor: Jerry Seinfeld says "Did you ever notice…"
Topical Humor: Jay Leno says "In the news today…"
Character Humor: Richard Pryor
Prop Humor: My NSA colleague Tim Gard, and Carrot Top
Physical Humor: Jim Carrey, Jerry Lewis
Impressionists: Kevin Pollack, Dana Carvey, and Mike Meyers
Improvisationalists: Robin Williams, Paula Poundstone

For years at my humor seminars, I've been sharing some funny stories that always seem to amuse people. Some of them are urban legends.

They are still just as funny. One of them is about a housewife who is doing the laundry. Her washer and dryer are located in the basement of her family's home. She takes a basketful of dirty laundry to the basement to put in the washer and decides to strip off her own clothing to add it to the load. She then removes a load of clean laundry from the dryer, puts it in the basket, and is about to walk up the basement steps with it when she notices that her son has left his football helmet on the steps. She picks up the helmet to take it to his room, but, having no other place to put it with both arms holding the laundry basket, she plunks it on her head. At that moment the outside basement door opens: it is the meterman who has come to read the meters, also located in the basement. The housewife drops the basket and stands exposed in the sunlight streaming in through the open doorway. The meterman gulps, and says, "I sure hope your team wins, lady." This story dates back to at least 1961, when a less scandalous version appeared in the pages of <u>Reader's Digest.</u>

Another story is about a lady who came home from the grocery store and she saw her husband working under the car. All that was exposed were his legs, so in passing she reached down, unzipped his zipper, chuckled to herself, and went into the house. Immediately she saw her husband sitting in the easy chair reading the newspaper. She cried, "Who is THAT under the car?" and her husband replied, "My mechanic." She told her husband what she'd done and they went outside to find the mechanic lying unconscious, because when the lady unzipped his pants he was so startled he sat up and clobbered his head under the car. Some seminar attendees told me they recall having first heard this legend as far back as the late 1950s.

Another story I heard at a humor conference was about a little preschooler who went to Walgreen's Pharmacy with his dad. As his dad picked up the prescription, the boy raised his hand to get the pharmacist's attention. The pharmacist said, "Yes son, what is it?" The boy asked "Do you have any tampons?" The pharmacist said "Tampons? What do you want them for?" The boy said, "Well, I saw a commercial on TV and with them it said you can swim and ride a bike; I can't do either of those things!"

Humorous situations are all around us and everywhere in the world. They're in books, audiotapes, movies, and daily interactions.

While I was in Israel, I boarded a city bus. I looked out the window and noticed a Palestinian mom with her three boys, aged about four, six and ten. The mom was giving each of them some chocolate. The four-year-old immediately crammed his mouth with chocolate, then looked at his six-year-old brother, grabbed his chocolate and crammed it into his stuffed mouth, as the shocked six-year-old, with jaw dropped, looked at him in disbelief and the ten-year-old fell to the ground cracking up laughing. As the bus drove off, I too was laughing. I enjoyed a humorous scene, because I had my eyes open for one. We can also see from this that it could have been me and my brothers or you and your siblings or friends. We all have much more in common than we do differences.

A great humorous comment can sustain a person for weeks. A bitter sarcastic comment can take weeks to get over. Therefore, choose laughter and choose Life! (Unless you have a different favorite cereal.)

Chapter Six:
Habit Four
Use the power of humor and its positive influence on yourself and others

Never underestimate your influence on others or the world as a whole. Here is a poem I wrote as an example of how we can be both powerful and insignificant at the same time:

I Forget Myself

I forget myself and
reach out across the canyon
changing the universe
in miraculous ways

I forget myself and
kiss the one I love
who should know that
I love without the kiss

I forget myself and
bless the ragged man
on the street corner
arm outstretched
crying for brotherhood

I forget myself and
correct the wanton child running
precariously close

to the frail older woman with frightened eyes

I forget myself and
volunteer to take up
the cause
knowing it is not
the practical thing to do

I forget myself and
compliment the person
that I thought to be my enemy

I forget myself and
take the time to really listen
to what another feels must be said

I forget myself and
honor my self

Then I remember myself
I am just a lazy human
with too many faults
full of self doubt
who will never attain greatness
in the eyes of the world

Then I forget myself
and reach out across
the canyon
changing the universe
in miraculous ways

The Old Testament references the healing properties of humor: "A merry heart doeth good like a medicine."[26]

---

[26] Proverbs 17:22, the Bible

Although our ancestors couldn't explain it scientifically, they knew intuitively that laughter was good for the body as well as the soul.

More recently, Norman Cousins, in <u>Anatomy of an Illness</u>[27], described how he used humor to help heal himself. Cousins reportedly watched old Marx Brothers movies, candid camera episodes and other funny tapes and laughed uncontrollably. He believes his own laughter played a significant role in overcoming his illness. He subsequently lived a long and healthy life – well into his 80s! Then he had a heart attack and died. What Norman said was true. Even though it was not scientifically investigated, I believe it to be more than just anecdotal, as it was personally true for me. When I cracked up for about ten minutes I could get two hours of pain-free sleep. Humor gave me the escape I needed to go on with my life. My sense of humor, which increased my ability to laugh, really helped to reduce the amount of pain pills I needed to take. I was able to tolerate pain better because of it. I did not necessarily have to crack up hearty to tolerate some extra pain, but rather get myself into the spirit of humor to "feel good." Laughter will have stronger physiological effects on pain, but even a smile helps. Use your sense of humor to experience joy on a daily basis. Sometimes the pain is a three to four on a one to ten scale and other days it's a seven or eight[28]. My goal was to increase the joy segments and decrease the pain levels. Humor does that for me. I put humorous things first and thus gave humor the power to transform my life. Other research has been done that concluded that more pain could be tolerated while watching humorous videos. Humor can also fight sickness. My evidence is anecdotal, but ask anyone in my household and they will verify that

---

[27] A book
[28] This has nothing to do with a sleep number bed®

9 out of 10 times that everyone in the house got sick, I did not. This is true even while I am on immunosuppressive drugs as well, not to mention the bugs and micro-shtoinks I was exposed to daily at the hospital. *(Micro-shtoinks are tiny shtoinks – shtoinks is a word my brother Phil invented that means… well, use your imagination.)*

Habit One is based on self-reflection and the ability to give things in life with the essential priority they deserve.

Habit Two is based on your self-confidence and self-esteem.

Habit Three reminds you to look for humor on a daily basis.

Habit Four reminds you that humor can be very powerful, even life transforming, if you're open to it.

I take TIME to enhance the lives of those important to me. Sacrificing for others is sacrificing for me.

This is not codependence. If there is a positive outcome to the interaction I have with others, this interaction makes my life richer. It is not the burnout do-for-others mentality that those caught in the codependent trap suffer. Is the action you take, in assisting others, energizing or draining? Sometimes only time can tell, but with this in mind you're on the right track.

Sharing your humor makes your day and the day of others better. That makes the world better.

One day my wife and I were arguing. Later that evening when I got into bed I figured she was over it. Guys can be dumb sometimes. As I went to cuddle with her, I heard this voice that sounded like the exorcist saying, "You're invading my legal side of the bed!" I went back over to my designated portion of the bed and a few minutes later she passed some gas. I said, "Your gas is invading my legal side of the bed!" With that we both laughed and cuddled to sleep. That is the power of humor. Humor can defuse angry situations. There are other things that it can't defuse though. Phyllis Diller said never go to bed angry – stay up and fight; well this was a better alternative.[29]

The personal humor strategies listed below can help influence yourself and others. They are actually tried and true strategies I have been using most of my life to increase the humor around me and its power.

The Silly Walk.

Using yourself physically gives you a kinesthetic experience that makes the humor a physical part of you. If you have seen Monty Python's <u>Dept. of Silly Walks</u> you'll get the idea of what I mean. Just choose some odd way of walking that amuses you. If you walk odd anyway, exaggerate it! Since my arthritis gave me a bad limp, I exaggerated it to the point of absurdity; this not only made me laugh and feel better, but also helped others get the message that I was comfortable with my illness, which eased their discomfort. I encourage you to amuse yourself while walking up and down stairs by moving your arms in awkward positions as you walk up or down. Please give it a try. I've been doing this for years and it never fails to bring a smile to my face.

Become an actor.

I touch on this in chapter 8, when I discuss the power of the humor spirit: Getting into the witness state. One way to do this is to become an actor for the moment. Choose an actor or character that you find amusing and funny. I chose Tevya

---

[29] My wife said, while reading this: "You apologize and say you'll never repeat this again and THEN you put it in a book!"

from the film <u>Fiddler on the Roof</u>. This technique is especially helpful when you find yourself becoming angry. If arguing or upset, "retake" the scene over with whomever you're having the conflict. I've done this many times. I would say something like "CUT! That could have won an academy award! Try repeating the same words with the same facial expression as you just did!" The person then becomes more conscious of their actions and behavior and can rarely repeat it as well. It becomes funny or at least less angry, bringing a new perspective on the situation: You are now an actor acting out a scene. This is very similar to a humorous fantasy. The idea is to use your imagination to create a visualization of yourself in a silly way to get you out of the strong emotions you are feeling at that particular moment.

Foreign accents.

You have to be very brave to try this one. Restaurants are my favorite place for this as the waiter/waitress will have no idea where you're from, but your friends know how you normally talk. I often keep it up through the whole meal. It's quite enjoyable. The phone is another place to use the accent. I have tried British, German, Israeli, Arabic, Irish, Scottish, Russian and many more. As kids, David Lempert and I did this as prank calls, but that was before caller ID.

Fake memo, policy, webpage, etc.

This can really be fun. It applies to work settings also:
This life is a test. It is only a test. If it had been an actual life, you would have received further instructions on where to go and what to do.

Memos around the hospital help to reduce stress around some controversial or unpopular polices, such as dress codes, etc.

One of my favorites is the legendary church bulletin. Here's a top ten list:

1. Don't let worry kill – let the church help!
2. Thursday night – Potluck supper. Prayer and medication to follow.
3. Remember in prayer the many who are sick of our church and community.
4. For those of you who have children and don't know it, we have a nursery downstairs.
5. This afternoon there will be a meeting in the South and North ends of the church. Children will be baptized at both ends.
6. Tuesday at 4 P.M. there will be an ice cream social. Will ladies giving milk please come early.
7. Wednesday the Ladies Literary Society will meet. Mrs. Jones will sing "Put Me In My Little Bed" accompanied by the Pastor.
8. Thursday at 5 P.M. there will be a meeting of the Little Mothers Club. All wishing to become Little Mothers please meet the Minister in his study.
9. On Sunday a special collection will be taken to defray the expenses of the new carpeting. All wishing to do something on the carpet, please come forward and get a piece of paper.
10. The ladies of the Church have cast off clothing of every kind. They may be seen in the basement on Friday afternoon.

The Humor Journal:

I have a humor journal that I have been keeping for many years. I suggest you start one. In it are my favorite one-liners, fake memos, stories, bumper stickers, and comic scenes that I have found funny or created myself.

Here are some entries:

How can you tell a social worker in a nudist camp? They're the one that's listening instead of looking.

My bumper sticker is on the honor roll at Bumper Sticker Grammar School

Personal arthritis flare-up humor – not meant to be shared, but I will share it for illustrative purposes: *"Why did the guy with arthritis fall down? Someone pushed him."*

Other humor journal excerpts:

"The doctor put me on an Ace-inhibitor due to high blood pressure, but I had to switch to a beta blocker because I kept losing at Black Jack."

David Jacobson

Three kids come down to the kitchen and sit around the breakfast table. The mother asks the oldest boy what he'd like to eat. "I'll have some $#%@! French toast," he says. The mother is outraged at his language, hits him, and sends him upstairs. She asks the middle child what he wants. "Well, I guess that leaves more f$#%@! French toast for me," he says. She is livid, smacks him, and sends him away. Finally she asks the youngest son what he wants for breakfast. "I don't know," he says meekly, "but I definitely don't want the $#%@! French toast."

"My brother Alan is considered well read. I travel a lot and listen to many talking books, but I'm not considered well heard. It's not fair."

"I don't deserve this award, but I have arthritis and I don't deserve that either."

Jack Benny

My grandfather always said, "Don't watch your money; watch your health." So one day while I was watching my health, someone stole my money. It was my grandfather."

Jackie Mason

Dolphins: Don't trust a species that's always smiling, its up to something!

I have always kept my guard up against becoming too arrogant. I did swallow my pride once, but it went down the wrong pipe.

"Humor is in my blood. Frankly, I wish it was in this book."

"I used to be a psychiatric social worker, but I wasn't crazy about it."

Five things to do when you're bored:
1. At lunchtime, sit in your parked car with sunglasses on and point a hairdryer at passing cars. See if they slow down.
2. Send e-mail to the rest of the company to tell them what you're doing. For example, "If anyone needs me, I'll be in the bathroom, in stall 3."
3. Specify that your drive-through order is "to eat here".
4. Every time someone asks you to do something, ask if they want fries with that.

1. When the money comes out of the ATM, scream, "I Won, I Won! Third time this week!!!"

Share embarrassing moments. Consider embarrassing moments; many are really funny. When something embarrassing happens to us, we feel mortified. I usually don't because I know I may have a new humorous story to tell. If you change the way you look at embarrassing moments, you will feel much less stress when they happen. This not only helps you overcome embarrassment, but gives others a good laugh too. My brother Phil shared an embarrassing situation with me that happened to him several years ago. He was in a store and picked up a <u>Playboy</u> magazine, opened it to the centerfold and nudged his wife, who was standing next him, and asked her, "what do you think of these?" The lady next to him wasn't his wife, but a seventy-year-old board member of the Jewish Community Center where he was the Director of Art. She looked at the picture and said, "Oh, that's nice."

I was visiting this same brother when he lived in Flagstaff, Arizona, along with my wife. As you know, I have psoriatic arthritis. Another chronic illness I have is … dun dun dun… the heartbreak of psoriasis. Sometimes this skin affliction affects sensitive parts of the body. That night as we were going to bed, my groin started to itch so I went to the medicine cabinet to see if Phil had anything in there I could sooth the itch with. I noticed a bottle of bactine and sprayed some on. It seemed to cool the area and I went off to bed. I awoke some time later in the night and felt a little burn in the area. I went back to the medicine cabinet and put some more bactine on and went back to bed. A few hours later I woke up with my groin area really burning. I sprayed more bactine on and couldn't go back to sleep. I lay there with the burn getting worse and worse. I tried to wait til morning but finally reached the point of going crazy at about 6 am. Laurie awoke to my jumping up and down holding my groin and yelling "I need to go to the hospital." This woke my brother and he took his car for us to follow him in ours to show us where the ER was. Laurie was driving and panicking because I was yelling OW! OW! OW! When we got there, other people were in the waiting room. The clerk started asking the insurance questions and stuff while I jumped up and down holding my groin and yelling for them to kill me or knock me out. The doctor finally gave me a shot. He then explained that I gave myself a chemical burn with the bactine and just kept making it worse by pouring more on. My brother says this story always reminds him of that Jerry Lee Lewis song, "Goodness Gracious!"

"And now for something completely different." Monty Python had it right with this statement. One thing an HHP does on a regular basis is something different. They take different routes to work. They eat different kinds of food. They vary their weekly routines. Doing any one of these things means you'll be doing one less negative thing. This provides you with a new way to see things rather than the usual boring or negative way. "Wow, instead of being stuck in traffic looking at the same old thing, I get to be stuck looking at completely different things!"

Habit four boils down to: If you can laugh at it, you can overcome it and if you can help others to laugh at their problems, they can overcome them too.

Chapter Seven:
Habit Five
Use your humorous imagination
to improve your communication

"Cohumorcation"

Humor is the affectionate communication of insight.
Leo C. Rosten

Mindscape
(To silly poetry: Inspired by the painting "Mindscape" by
Philip Rubinov Jacobson)

The mindscape where
I label my thoughts

good
bad
ugly
Clint Eastwood
How did he get here?
in the mindscape
of my thoughts
I am more than
a fistful of dollars

What does this poem mean? Does it have to mean anything? If the poem puts me in a better mood it has served its purpose by changing my mood for the better, which opens me to better hear others and be more open to communication.

This poem has everything to do with using humor to improve your communication skills. Mis-communication happens more often than Mr-communication. The ability to clarify communication has much to do with your mental state at the time of the communication. If you hate the bastard you're speaking to, then chances are you'll not be too concerned with what he/she has to say. Oops, the he/she does not necessarily imply a transgendered person, although it could; it could also be an actual person who is a he or a she. See how easy miscommunication happens? Actually it does have something to do with gender as apparently, according to a source known to me, I was born on Mars and my wife was born on Venus, which explains why my kids act like aliens a lot of the time. See, even here miscommunication is present. John Gray never stated that anyone's birthplace has anything to do with anything he said. He said men are *from* Mars, not born there. Here's another example. Back in my college days I was at my friend's house. Her grandfather was in the back yard yelling. I couldn't see, but I heard, so I ran back there as it was not a very safe neighborhood and I was a little concerned that he was being murdered or assaulted or something. I asked him, "What's wrong?" In his thick Ukrainian accent he said, "Some dam kyats just ran through the backyard and jumped over the fence." My friend came out and asked what was wrong. I explained about the cats running through the yard and over the fence. She started laughing. "What's so funny?" I asked. She said, "he meant kids not cats."

Here are some cohumorcation (communicating with a humorous perspective) tips:

Tip One: Use your humorous imagination to improve your listening skills.

Lets say that you are angry with another person you are about to speak to. This will make communication with them very difficult. You must get out of the angry mood. Think to yourself something along the lines of: "I wonder what this person would do if cheese started pouring out of their ear?" The other person will then see you smiling and know you are open to communication. You will feel better and be more willing to listen. You will be "listening with humor."

Tip Two: Pretend what you are about to hear is the most important thing you will ever hear in your life. When you are that focused on someone, they will think you are the most wonderful person in the world. Try it and you will be very surprised at the positive results.

Tip Three: Caring is the key. It has to come from within. Not caring enough is usually the reason for poor communication.

Let me give you another example. My wife Laurie says to me, "Honey, how do baked chicken breasts sound for dinner?" But I hear, "Will you pour honey on my breasts?"

Why does this happen? Is it a male/female thing?

Is it a Mars and Venus thing or perhaps a mouth and ear thing? Yes, it is all of these.

Guys, we just don't listen the same way the gals do. What about sexual orientation? Do gay men listen better? I don't think so, but I could be wrong.

It has to do with how hard one is willing to work at listening. Communication is hard work. It seems that more men are lazier than women are when it comes to that department. Yes, there are poor female listeners and good male listeners. But generally speaking, guys do a poor job at it, myself included.

Here is an excerpt from a conversation with my wife, also known as one of the best listeners on the planet. She is much better at it than I am.

Laurie: "I know how to listen."
David: "How do you know how to listen?"
Laurie: "Because I pay attention. I put my heart into it."
David: "Why?"
Laurie: "Because I'm interested."
David: "Why are you interested?"
Laurie: "Because I care."

Laurie: "Where are you going?"
David: "To the store to get honey."
Laurie with a confused look: "Why?"
David: "You know" (*sly smile on my face*).

Communication is one of the most important skills in life. Why did I choose social work as my profession? A helping profession like nursing? Because my humorgy requires of me that I help others. Humor helps people help people.

My undergraduate major in college was sociology, where I learned about an experiment called The Good Samaritan Study. Isen and Levin of the University of California at Berkeley carried out this study.

The subjects were callers from public pay phones in malls in San Francisco and Philadelphia. Some subjects found a dime in the pay phone (planted there by the experimenters), while others did not. As each subject left the phone booth, a confederate of the experimenter dropped a folder full of papers in his or her path.

Of the eight men and eight women who had found the free dimes, six men and eight women helped the confederate pick up her papers.

Of the nine men and sixteen women who had not found a free dime, eight men and sixteen women did not help the confederate pick up the papers.

Social psychologists Isen and Levin suggest that finding the dime led subjects to be in a good mood, and feeling good leads to helping. See how being an HHP can help make the world a better place? What I want to know is: Are there still confederates alive today and does the fact that these experiments took place in the north affect how many people help the confederates?

If you see me smile while explaining your "stance," even if you disagree with me, you will feel I am really listening and rather than coming from a place of judgment or anger, I'm coming from a place of joy.

> "So I'd like to know where you got the notion,
> said I'd like to know where you got the notion
> to rock the boat, don't rock the boat baby
> rock the boat, don't tip the boat over
> rock the boat, don't rock the boat baby
> rock the boat-t-t-t-t."

This song is filled with inherent contradictions. Communication can get like that.

Which boat is right? We get caught up with "our boat." Our boat consists of the baggage, judgments, projections and perceptions we give higher power to than even our loved ones. This is ass backwards. These bags, judgments, projections and perceptions hold us back from truly hearing others. Use humor to break through these barriers to communication. Overcoming these barriers will improve your relationships and all your interactions with others. The amount of stress in you life will decrease and the amount of health and joy will increase.

Please do me a big favor. Close your eyes. I know you can't read with your eyes closed, so open them when you have to read the next instruction, but then close them again. Picture a boat in the water. Get as detailed a picture as possible. Is it moving? What color is it? What type of boat is it? How big is it? What is the water like?

NOW, here's the clincher. If someone else is thinking of a different boat, is his or her boat wrong and yours right? Can they both be right for each of you? Why do we get caught up with needing to have others tell us that our boat is right? This is the basis of most arguments. Instead of boats, it is our values or politics or religion. I can smile while you describe your boat. When you reach a point when you can smile when someone else is describing their "boat" you have mastered humorous communication and thus basic communication. When you can laugh with someone of another religion, political party or with different values, you have obtained the ability to "humorize," which will be explained in detail in the next chapter.

Republican, Democrat, Christian, Jew, Muslim, Buddhist, Hindu. Gay, Straight, Metro-sexual, whatever the hell that is. They're all different colored boats. One is not right and one is not WRONG! In an M&M bag® there are greens, reds, browns, yellows. I don't think there are whites though? Wow, that is one of the only analogies that leaves whites out. Isn't that cool? All the M&Ms taste good. If you closed your eyes, you would not be able to tell which color M&M you just ate. A master of "humorgy" is like that. They don't look for a "color" (value, religion, political party, gender preference, etc.), they savor the taste. We all have different tastes. We have different tastes in humor like we do in food. There is not a right and wrong taste. When you can embrace the differences, you will decrease the amount of judgment and prejudice in the world.

Humorous listening (cohumorcation) diffuses anger. It decreases stress. It helps us become more flexible.

This will help make the world a better place for all of us. *I want to make it clear that I am talking about tolerance. I can tolerate someone with a different viewpoint, but they have a responsibility to – as they say in the Hippocratic oath – "Do no harm." Tolerance does not mean condoning irresponsible behavior.* A strong humor foundation gives you the confidence to listen to another's point of view. You do not have to agree with it.

We all have fears. We don't want others to make us change our minds or worldviews. If you are confident and open you can go from the "Yes, but" mentality to the "Yes, and" mentality.

Let's embrace and enjoy all the boats in the world. Even an environmentalist can understand that though some boats increase pollution, they can also have a positive impact. For example, a large sailboat filled with biodegradable environmental literature can help educate many ignorant people. Don't try to analyze this. It is supposed to be humorous. Everyone knows that when you analyze humor, it dies in the process.

Take the time and do the hard work of truly communicating. Communicate with your mind, heart and spirit. Give the time needed in order to truly understand

and you will save much more time than you could ever imagine. Do it with joy and you'll get an added benefit. So will the person or people you're communicating with.

Use humor to overcome the following barriers to communication:

Ways negative self-communicated thoughts seep into our minds.

Magnification and Minimization: I wrestled in high school and won every match in the 127 weight group and lost every match in the 134 weight group (when I wrestled over my normal weight). This was a pretty even split. If I magnify every match in the higher weight and minimize every one at my normal weight I will feel like a loser and negative thoughts will prevail. If I do the opposite, positive thoughts and feelings will prevail.

Emotional Reasoning: Making decisions based on emotions rather than reason. I'll never sell one copy of this book once it's done, so why should I even try to finish it. I'm not smart enough to make this into a good book. "Negative Emotional Reasoning Detracts" from your highly humorous abilities. This acronym for NERD can keep you down. The opposite choice for NERD can also be chosen: "Normal Everyday Right Decisions." Everyone has acted like an idiot at one time or another, be relieved when your turn is done. "Normal everyday right decisions" can also prevail.

Being Full of Shoulds: I should have done that instead of this. I should have been more of this than that. I should have known better. Why? Your psychic abilities are not working right? Your Supreme Being normal perfection is faltering? Why should you be perfect? A better question: Why on earth do you think, as a human, you should be above making mistakes?

Labeling and Mislabeling: What a lazy bum I am. Why am I so lazy? I never work hard. I never have worked hard and never will. Reality: I have had bouts of laziness and bouts of hard work. I will not label myself based on the most negative times of my life.

Personalization: My kids are not perfect, I must have gone wrong somewhere.

Maybe my kids have to go through childhood in their own way. Maybe they will make their own choices no matter what I advise them. Don't take other's moods and perceptions personally. There's a lot more to the picture than oversimplifying like that.

Below is a poem about communication between my self and my love.

A Picnic in the Cemetery
(Inspired by "The Picnic" by Philip Rubinov Jacobson)

A lazy Sunday afternoon, we awaken late after a long
    restful sleep
Our cloudy day to do nothing, turns into a day to remember

With a bottle of wine in hand and blanket over my shoulder
And the bag with cheese, chips and chicken in your hand

We stroll around the cemetery, to the old woodsy section
    of the civil war era
Up the small hill we lay the blanket on the thick soft mushy
    grass

Your eyes touching mine, warms the cool fall day
as we partake in our bounty, enjoying each other's chewing
    faces

The crumpled bag of leftovers and the empty bottle lay
    near our resting bodies
Safe, soothed and drifting off, we watch the dipping sun

A sprinkle of rain, are tears of love as they touch us
We feel their wet kisses and we collapse into each other's
    hearts

Content with this fading day, we smile
Knowing we have created the memory

Of a picnic in the cemetery

This poem communicates the importance of creating positive memories for future times to think back on and enjoy.

Both love and humor in communication can defuse anger and resolve conflict. Humor that comes from a place of love is humor in its highest form. Playful humor can improve interpersonal communication.

The more specific you can be about the type of HHP you want to be, the more highly skilled you will become in that specific type of humor. For example, if you say, "I want to have more humor," you may end up with a lot of aqueous humor, which isn't the type of humor you may be after.

More specific would be, "I want to be an expert at parody." You may end up the next Weird Al Yankovich, who to my knowledge has not yet been parodied.

Chapter Eight:
Habit Six
Humorize With Humorgy
The power of the humor spirit

Humor can be very powerful, even life transforming, if you're open to it.

"When one door of happiness closes, another one opens; but often we look so long at the closed door that we do not see the one which has opened for us."

Helen Adams Keller

For your reading pleasure, I will now attempt to explain what I mean by these terms using various illustrations, examples and definitions. This will help you better understand the meanings of humorgy and humorize. To humorize is to have the ability, when you are in a poor mood, to merely think about something funny and begin to feel better. A person who can humorize with ease is an HHP. They have mastered the half habit of changing the negative into the positive. Laughter normally occurs unconsciously. It is easier to inhibit laughter than to laugh on command. To humorize with humorgy means you have the ability to consciously produce laughter. Laughter is largely still a mystery. We have only just begun to explore this uncharted realm of the mind. This is why explaining "humorgy" or "humorize" is so difficult. It is taking a universal, but very personal experience and trying to put into words – something felt on a spiritual and emotional level in addition to its physiological, psychological and social levels.

When you can humorize with humorgy, you can appreciate everyone's "boat." Your humor self and your spiritual self become one and the same. Like putting food coloring into water, once done, the food coloring powder cannot be separated out. You've colored your spirit with your humor and have enhanced it. This improves your ability to infuse humor into the world. Someone who can humorize with humorgy can better appreciate love, hope, joy and all the other positive emotions. People that humorize with humorgy see that judging is useless, revenge is futile, resistance to the spirit of humor is futile, and arguing with a Borg is futile. Your life and everyone you come in contact with is worth more than petty thoughts. Imagine being able to see something from your perspective and from an opposing perspective at the same time. To humorize with humorgy is to do just that. It's like Tevya when he sees one perspective and another and agrees they are both right and then hears a third opinion. For example:

Person One: "Why should I break my head about the outside world? Let the outside world break its own head."

Tevya: "Well put! He is right. As the Good Book says, "If you spit in the air, it lands in your face. "
Person Two: "Nonsense. You can't close your eyes to what's happening in the world."
Tevya: "He is right."
Person Three: "He's right and he's right? They can't both be right."
Tevya: "You know, you are also right."[30]

If you have two cups and one has a hole in it, which one would you put your colored water in? Putting water in the cup with the hole is like trying to pour your opinions into another person with different opinion cups. We all do this every day. I am not talking about sharing our opinions, I'm talking about trying to force your opinions (colored water) into another person's cup (spirit). "My faith is better than your faith. "My values are superior to yours." "My opinions are more valid than yours." It's all nonsense. Rather than try to change the other person, share your cup of colored water with them. Let them taste your flavor. Don't pour your flavor into their cup! Humorgy allows one to appreciate their own value and the values of others. Friendship should be based on nothing more than – if it feels right, then it's a good relationship. Some exceptions to this is if the relationship is with a serial killer and you don't know it, or if it involves deceit with another relationship. Other than that, it's a pretty good guide to follow.

By combining humor with all other aspects of life, your entire lifestyle will change. To humorize is to have the ability to look at yourself and pull your pain out of the driver's seat and place it in the back seat. The greater your pain, the greater will be your ability to humorize. This is

---

[30] Fiddler on the Roof

why some people who are extremely funny have overcome extreme tragedies in their life.

Take all parts of you – your spiritual self, your physical self, your mental self, your social self, your economic self, and your political self.

When you can take all parts of yourself and add the spirit of humor you experience wholeness in a way that can't be described, only felt. Be open to that and you'll have humorgy. With humorgy you see the whole, which diminishes prejudice, judgment, and all negative aspects of life. Humor reveals the interconnection between all of us. It is an ideal that we can all strive to reach. When you master habit six and are able to humorize with humorgy you can actually control, to a certain extent, the spirit of humor discussed in the beginning. You will have mastered humorgy. Humorgy can be used for self-control. Those humorous thoughts protect you from getting sucked into the vacuum cleaner of dirt, hate, anger, depression, envy, greed, jealousy and other deadly sins.

Electric River

(To the human mind)
Inspired by the painting, "Electric River" by Philip
Rubinov-Jacobson

Within my brain
flows an electric river
sending pulses I interpret wrongly
as pulses
rather than simply existing
as pure form
words
killing
any self-examination
as soon as written
waves of thought forms
deciphering, changing, redirecting
the electric rivers course
to freeze the surge
for an instant
is this poems goal
don't think
don't write
don't read
simply be
Electric River

The "electric river" is one essential portion of humorgy, the others being spirit, consciousness, emotion and some other esoteric thing that I can't think of right now.

Perhaps you can use your humorgy to come up with whatever the other thing is.

My wife, Laurie, looked at the word humorgy and said, "Gee that looks like a combination of humor and orgy." When I think of it, she may be right; if you define the term orgy by its definition of being excessive in something to satisfy an inordinate appetite or craving. A humor orgy or humorgy is an unending craving for humor. If you have to be addicted to something, I recommend an addiction to humor. It is one of the only addictions that can alter your consciousness without damaging your health, and can actually improve your health.

To be able to humorize with humorgy is an underexplored area of "Psychoneurospirituimmunology." The actual word that my made-up word is based on is psychoneuroimmunology (PNI), but the spiritual component is so important that it deserves a part in defining any holistic approach to healing.

PNI defines the communication links and relationships between our emotional experience and our immune response as mediated by the neurological system. Robert Ader, a psychiatrist on the faculty at the University of Rochester, coined the term in 1975. Psychoneuroimmunology is the study of the interactions among the behavioral, neural and endocrine (or neuroendocrine), and immunological processes of adaptation. It's a relatively new field of the mind, body, and spirit connections, but researchers haven't found a way to put the spirit under a microscope yet so they leave that part out. As discussed in our half habit, our behaviors and thoughts can effect and modify immune functions. Scientists are discovering what yogis have known for centuries. We can control our heart rate, our blood pressure, our body heat, our digestion and a whole bunch of other previously thought involuntary body functions of our autonomic system. In addition, "Yogis" also have known how pleasurable picnic baskets are. "Boo Boos" would also agree with this. Where does the spiritual aspect fit in? There is not much literature on this topic. There is no definitive definition of spiritual humor. It is as diverse as the number of religious and spiritual orders in the universe. This makes it difficult to measure. It's not like economics where you can say 84% of struggling or lost souls are due to lack of humor, etc.

I have a humorous relationship with what I call "The Master of the Universe." It is not sacrilegious but highly religious to me to jest with "the master of the universe." It's obvious he/she has a sense of humor or I would never have been created. My life is a joke and I mean that in the most sacred way. Hopefully you feel the same. Anyone who has made it this far in the book is likely to have a similar philosophy of life.

There are so many times in my life and yours that we run across examples of the cosmic joke. One example is the teeth on the steering wheel story.[31] When I got to the church that morning to give that humor and spirituality talk, I retold the story of what happened on the way, ending with me biting that steering wheel. It was a cloudy, rainy day. At the end of the story I said to the congregation, "You know, every once in a while we get confirmation from above that we are doing what we should be doing." Just then, BAM! A huge thunder crack sounded! I looked up to the ceiling and said "THANK YOU!" Another example of the cosmic joke: I have been to Israel three times. On each return to Rochester, my best friend, David, picked me up at the airport. Each time we got in the car David put the radio on and the song "The Boys are Back in Town" by Thin Lizzy would be playing on the radio. All those strange but true stories are in fact strange, but true. Whether you believe in a higher power or not, it's hard to deny that there is something going on there, and it's funny too. Funny and strange have often been used interchangeably. I'm a funny guy. I'm also a strange guy. People that think I'm strange don't realize

---

[31] page 31

I'm just being funny and people that think I'm being funny, don't realize I'm just being strange.

As a spiritual being I am having fun trying to figure out the unfathomable while in this body. How can you live life as a drudge when there is such a limited time on this planet? If I had a thousand years, okay, I'd be serious for maybe a hundred years, but that's not the case. John Milton Fogg defined belief as "being in love" with an idea or concept. I love that interpretation. Be in love with the idea that the creator of the world exists in whatever form you choose to believe in. Be in love with the idea that you have a cooperative part and influence in that master plan created by the creator of the universe. The greatest definition I have found for spiritual humor is in the movie The Meaning of Life by Monty Python.[32] In it Eric Idle sings a song called the "Galaxy Song." It is a great "revelation" of the spiritual explanation to the phrase "the cosmic joke of the universe."

One contradiction of the cosmic joke is that as small as we feel, we also feel that we have universal potential at the same time to create great outcomes that can affect our universe as well.

We are the heroes of our own lives. We all have heroes that reflect and "prove' to us that this is true and how our heroes, many of whom we've never met or who may have been dead corpses for centuries, have influenced us as we in turn have influenced others. Woody Allen's humor has influenced me: "Two old ladies are in a restaurant. One complains, 'You know, the food here is just terrible.' The other shakes her head and adds, 'And such small portions.' Steve Wright – "I knew these Siamese twins. They moved to England, so the other one could drive." Robin Williams – "If it's the Psychic Network, why

---

[32] The Meaning of Life ,1983, directed by Terry Jones and Terry Gilliam.

do they need a phone number?" Billy Crystal – "Women need a reason to have sex. Men just need a place." Steve Allen – "My wife and I had words, but I never got to use mine!" The Marx brothers – "When I invite a woman to dinner I expect her to look at my face. That's the price she has to pay!" The list goes on and on.

One of the reasons that I can walk today is because of people I have never met and may never meet. I do have a better chance now since I have mentioned them in my book.[33]

Integral parts of "psychoneurospirituimmunology." When we combine the elements below, we have a human being with a high level of humorgy that is greater than the sum of each of these separate individual parts (the mind, the physical self and the spiritual self).

1. Our thought processes: "I am great and can overcome obstacles."
2. Our physical bodies: "I feel healing energy in my body."
3. Our nervous system: "I feel warm without wetting my pants."
4. Our spiritual selves: "I have a reason for being here."

There is a well-known story about a Texas billionaire who held a big bash every year. He would always have some outrageous event to highlight the evening. At this year's event he filled his Olympic-sized swimming pool full of man-eating (and women-eating) alligators and announced, "Anyone who dares to swim the length of this pool and survives to make it out the other side can have either a million dollars, half my estate, or the hand of my daughter in marriage." With that, everyone heard a splash at the end of the pool. A man was swimming, kicking and punching alligators. Amazingly, he made it out alive on

---

[33] I prefer to meet the living ones.

the other side. "Do you want a million dollars?" asked the billionaire. "No!" he replied. "Do you want half my estate?" The man responded, "Of course not." The billionaire said, "I suppose you want my daughter's hand?" "NO! What would I do with your daughter's hand?" The billionaire, frustrated at this point said, "Well, what do you want?" The man replied, "I want to find the SOB who pushed me in the pool!"

In everyone's life there comes a time when we find ourselves in that pool. Whether we're pushed in, fall in, or choose to jump in doesn't matter much. The important thing is to find a way out before drowning or being eaten alive. Humorgy is your life jacket to help you survive while in the pool and the rod to pull you out before it's too late.

A moment I had an insight due to humorgy:

When I was first diagnosed with severe arthritis, I dropped fifteen pounds in two weeks. You wouldn't think it takes energy to eat, but it can under certain circumstances. It was a great effort to even chew and shallow food. When you are in a critical condition, eating can become a monumental task. I didn't even have the strength to raise my body up in bed. It took weeks to become strong enough to get into a wheelchair and return to the USA from Israel, where I had gotten sick. Walking was excruciatingly painful. I was twenty-two and just beginning to walk all over again. If you're familiar with the character Edith Bunker on "All in the Family," you know who my mom is. I get the eerie feeling that Jean Stapleton turned invisible and followed my mother around the house for months to study her before she developed the Edith Bunker character. My mother, like Edith, is extremely popular because she is the sweetest person in our family. She is unconditionally loving to everyone she knows and also manages to keep high spirits even when she is facing a tragedy. Her name is Rose. Now, any normal twenty-two-year-old should dread moving back home after just obtaining their independence. If you are forced to ever return home at the age of twenty-two, just go to Rose's house and it will be a more pleasant experience. In fact, she has taken in many a strays over the years; people who have been abandoned by their families. She was very helpful to me upon my return in such a debilitated state. I left the USA as a healthy 130 pound guy and returned as a 110 pound skeleton. Rose was very helpful. She was overly helpful, running to get the phone (imagine Edith Bunker's voice), *"...Oh, don't get up David, I'll get it!"* Doing the laundry and asking, *"What do you want for dinner Archie and David?"* Actually there was no Archie. My mother never remarried since the death of her husband when she was forty-two years old (now, more than forty years ago). I knew she would do everything for me. What I really needed at that point was to gain as much independence as possible. I did not plan on becoming permanently disabled, totally dependent on others. I came up with a plan to get back on my feet. My first step was literally a humorous one. My plan was to beat her to the phone. This was an almost impossible feat considering how fast she moved and how slowly I dragged my painful feet. Humor can be very powerful, even life transforming. This was a life transforming moment for me. What I did that day forever changed the course of my future. It was a Sunday afternoon in December of 1980. It was minus 5 degrees out, a rather warm day for Rochester. I waited for that phone to ring. It finally happened. "Ring, ring." "Ring, ring." Rose called out, "Don't get up, I'll get it!" I said to my mother, "No, wait! I'll get it!" I kind of dragged myself like Igor, on the knuckles of my right hand touching the floor, drooling, tongue out and hobbling toward the phone. She was so busy laughing that I beat her to the telephone. At that moment, the secret humorgy revealed to me was that the thoughts in my head affected my mood, which in turn affected my perspective. This insight was what prompted the creation of the first "half habit." Even with the excruciating pain of my severe arthritis, I could still have fun. I could still laugh. I could smile at my own idiocies. I could have fun thoughts replace the fearful and depressing ones. There are certain prerequisites to experiencing the humor force. First you must have the ability to think. You must also have a brain to decipher the thought. Add some spirit, soul, senses, language, gravy and potatoes and the potential for the humor force is present.

There is increasing research that reveals the connection of your thoughts, moods, emotions, and belief system and your body's health and healing abilities.

By increasing the amount of humor in situations I experience today, I increase the number of happy memories I will have tomorrow and how quickly I become a more highly humorous person in the future.

In the moment that the humor force takes over, you go into the witness state of humorgy.

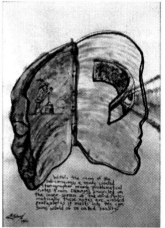

The Witness 1972 Philip Rubinov-Jacobson

This means getting out of yourself to see the situation from a different perspective. Humor can give you the amazing power to do just that – to see through humorgy-filtered eyes with a new, fresh, better, more positive perspective.

If you've ever seen <u>Fiddler on the Roof</u>, they showed Tevya going into the 'witness state.' Whenever he's got to make a decision, everything would freeze, and then he'd say, "Hum, let's look at this side of it..., on the other hand there is this..., on the other hand there is this side again."

When you're emotionally involved in a situation, it's difficult to be objective or positive about it. With humor you can separate yourself from it, get a distance, see the humor and become more objective in order to find a positive resolution.

Obi-Wan KaDavid and Darth David: An internal conversation about the first laugh between my mother and I after my return home (the phone ringing incident) and beginning to walk my first steps again.

Darth David: "Your life is over. (*Heavy breathing sound*) If you were dead you would not have to live in extreme pain everyday." (*Heavy breathing sound*)

Obi-Wan KaDavid: "Oh kiss my twenty-two-year-old arthritic behind. You don't know what you're talking about. I had fun today. I saw my mother laugh for the first time since I came home in this crippled body. I laughed for the first time since I got home."

Darth David: (*heavy breathing sound*) "Yeah, well you'll never run again, never compete in an athletic event again. Never have a pain free body again. Never..."

Obi-Wan KaDavid (interrupting Darth David): "Humor changed my life today. I'm not going back to YOU.

Your days are over and you're just trying to pull me down. It won't work, go away."

Darth David: "Oh, okay, (*heavy breathing sound*) but if you ever want to be depressed again, just let me know. Bye!"

Obi-Wan KaDavid: "Bye."

Just as in the Force, there is a dark side to humor. One aspect of the dark side of humor is inappropriate humor.

Exercise: What does your dark side say to you? Think of some common negative self-talk statements you find yourself thinking.

How can you use your humorgy to counter?

We have all heard of synergy and no one really knows what that means, but most have a vague idea. Humorgy is in the spiritual realm of humor. Humorgy is to synergy as joy is to life. Don't try to think about that too hard. Humorgy is the combined effect of understanding every aspect related to humor incorporated into your worldview. The words humorgy and the humor force are synonymous. I apologize for repeating myself, but I want to get used to doing it, so when I am even older, I already know how to do it right. Some parts of humorgy include jokes, play, laughter, wit, sarcasm, exaggeration, surprise, and the list goes on and on. We have acquired our humor knowledge through our senses, culture and personal experiences. Additionally, there are invisible and "unknowable" aspects of humor that play a part in humorgy. Some elements are on a subconscious level. For example, your humor spirits nature. Let's say you're reading this sentence and suddenly you remember the funniest thing that ever happened in your life. The force of humor overtakes you and you smile and feel warm. You do not feel warm because you just wet your pants, but because there is something unknowable involved and as such, unexplainable. The part of humor that is unexplainable in words, but present and felt during laughter, play, etc., is the spirit of humor. According to Humor Spirit Theory, the resulting warm feeling derived from the spirit of humor can be sensed through the whole of your being. Jumping in a hot tub can give you a warm feeling also, but a hot tub is usually not available at the time you are in need of a warm feeling. When you are smiling and feeling that warm feeling, you feel good, but can't explain why. In that moment you are experiencing humorgy. If you happen to be in a hot tub at the time of experiencing humorgy you feel doubly warm.

Sometimes observing someone cracking up and attempting to tell you about the funny occurrence is enough to get you to smile or laugh yourself, without even knowing why they are laughing.

As we learn more about humor, our perception of humor changes, thus changing our perception of humor can dramatically improve our sense of humor.

Our lives can be rich when our pockets are poor.

It's the choice to enjoy it that makes us want more.

You may set up your own funny situation and take a picture of it. It can provide a lot of laughs when you do so, and even more laughter afterward when everyone looks at the pictures.

Chapter Nine:
Habit Seven
Act like the highly humorous person you've become or are becoming

Now that you are on your journey to becoming an HHP, continue on your journey to ever-increasing humorgy. Use your advanced humor powers to help others further improve their sense of humor. Take more time to laugh, watch a comedy, see some stand-up, act silly, etc.

Honor your highly humorous self. Even if you're not quite there yet, if you act as an HHP, you become one much more quickly.

To be an HHP you must take on the personality of an HHP. When responding to situations, respond as an HHP would. Consider self-thoughts such as, "If I were an HHP, I would probably respond like this…"

By responding like an HHP, you are putting out the message to the universe that you intend to become more and more of an HHP.

When you're acting as if you're an HHP, you eliminate oppositional, negative self-talk. Acting like an HHP means you are trying to see the world like an HHP would and are more likely to discover views that an HHP would. You'll begin behaving, thinking and taking on the habits of an HHP. With the help of this book, others you know and additional resources, you will be capable, knowledgeable, and skillful enough to be one. The more you act like one, the more powerful your humor force will become and you will begin to act like an HHP automatically.

Results of being highly humorous include improved self-confidence, better self-esteem, and the ability to handle higher amounts of stress, be less phased by irritations and have a stronger immune system and improved mental health.

What makes highly humorous people different? I have found that what makes me different than most wasn't any incredible willpower. I have no superhuman ability to tolerate pain. I am not a genius. One thing to keep in mind is that there are a lot of intelligent people out there who are not highly humorous. There are a lot of depressed wealthy people out there. There are even a lot of depressed successful people out there. What made me different, I discovered, was my daily thoughts are much different than those of others. These are the highly humorous thoughts of the half habit. Do you try to think of silly things every day? Do you try to see the absurdities of life in all your interactions? If you did, you would be so much healthier it would be incredible. One clarification – happiness and healthiness are related, but not the same thing. I am not saying, "Don't worry. Be happy!" although I believe strongly in that philosophy. What I am saying is, take your negative thoughts, your painful problems with living on this planet and try to twist them around into something silly. When you become an HHP, you are able to change the thoughts that depress you. The messages you tell yourself of what a tortured life you have, how depressing your situation is and how things may never get better can change into something else.

An HHP has humility.

My humor has helped me come from a place of gratefulness. Seeing what a joke I am as a human has humbled me to the point of really appreciating what I have.

An HHP laughs from their source.

If we laugh only from our mouths and add nothing from our hearts then the laughter is lacking the spirit of humor. After we have had a good laugh, as beautiful as it can be, there may linger in our hearts some precious sentiments of joy emoted from the laughter, which we are unable to express outwardly.

This is the laughter that comes from the joy of our most intimate feelings and thoughts. And yet, we may not be able to find the words for their expression. Thoughts that lie too deep for words may be expressed by our silent smile. Some of our deepest joys never find expression in words, they remain in the realm of our humor spirit.

A great poet has written: "Heard melodies are sweet, but those unheard are sweeter." From time to time we have heard melodies which play not upon the ear, but within our humor spirit, and melodies which originate not outside ourselves but in the innermost part of ourselves. I have seen smiles on faces that have revealed these innermost melodies, music from the spirit of humor.

An HHP experiences humorgy on the deepest level.

Music from our humor spirit emerges out of our inner depths – created by our fears and our hopes, by our guilt and our gratitude, by our needs and our aspirations. The cathartic release of these inner melodies gives rise to a level of awareness of spiritual connections that goes beyond the limited understanding of the mind. Could you ever put into words the feeling of collapsing into uncontrollable laughter and the feeling it blanketed you with during its occurrence? You could not, but you could smile and nod to another who has experienced the same thing.

HHPs act as if their first choice of response to many situations is a humorous one. Earlier in this book I mentioned belief.[34]

Believe that you are a highly humorous person. Be in love with the idea that you can change the course of yours and others lives by your use of humor.

Acting is a form of practicing. There is a difference between pretending to be something and practicing to be something through your actions.

The principles laid out in this book are my principles.

And as Groucho Marx said: "Those are my principles, and if you don't like them...well, I have others."

The majority of people in this country are not highly humorous. In fact only one out of every five people in the US ever even make an attempt to become highly humorous. A survey conducted by the U.S. census bureau has concluded that these one out of five people make up only 20% of the population.

There's an old story about Buddha talking to a hot dog stand vendor. He did not know that the vendor was a highly humorous person (he may have been just acting as if he was, though). Buddha said to the hot dog vendor, "Make me one with everything." The vendor made him one with everything and said, "That'll be two dollars. Buddha gave him a five dollar bill. The vendor smiled and sat back down. Buddha asked, "Where's my change?" The hot dog vendor replied, "Change must come from within."

Through these habits, the changes you make will help you to become more humorous.

As my gnome Chuckles once said: "The journey of one thousand laughs begins with one chuckle." What are you waiting for? Start chuckling!

---

[34] page 80

Appendix B

(Appendix A removed due to emergency surgery.)

Resources and recommendations for further information. This section is written to replace the "Appendix A" which had to be removed due to emergency surgery. The "Tonsils" section also had to go.

The following books and sources have influenced me. They are highly recommended.

Humor at Work by Esther Blumenfeld and Lynne Alpern
How to Be Funny by Steve Allen
The Seven Habits of Highly Effective People by Stephen Covey
Lighten Up: Survival Skills for People under Pressure by C.W. Metcalf, 1994
Humor, Healing, and the Amuse System: Humor as Survival Training by Paul McGhee, 1996, Dubuque, Iowa: Kendall/Hunt Publishing
Don't Worry, He Won't Get Far on Foot by John Callahan
The Feeling Good Handbook by David Burns, 1989, New York: William Morrow
An Essay on Laughter by James Sully, 1902.
Humor, Its Origin and Development by Paul McGhee, 1979, San Francisco, Freeman
Treasury of Humor by Isaac Asimov
Brain Droppings by George Carlin
Every book ever written by Dave Barry
Every book ever written by Woody Allen
Every book ever written by Mark Twain

The Hitchhiker's Guide to the Galaxy series by Douglas
    Adams
Still Life with Woodpecker by Tom Robbins
The Comedy Bible by Judy Carter

Recommended movies:
When you need a lift, watch one of these….

Parenthood
The Family Guy
Oh Brother, Where Art Thou?
Tootsie
Dr. Strangelove or: How I learn to stop worrying and love
    the bomb
Blazing Saddles
The Producers
Mr. Destiny
It's a Wonderful Life
The Meaning of Life
Fear and Loathing in Las Vegas
It's a Mad Mad Mad Mad world
All Marx Brothers movies

For additional picks go to this link:
http://www.afi.com/tvevents/100years/laughs.aspx

My website: http://www.humorhorizons.com

Gall Bladder A
This section may have to be removed, it must be observed for a while first before a final clinical decision is made.

What would you say, if you had something that you felt someone must know before you go? Do you want your last night spent in front of the TV or next to someone you love who is watching TV?

Actually taking time to hear that which a loved one wants to tell you or you want to tell them is a good way to use a little time.

If you knew you had one more sneeze, would you try to hold it in or be as loud as possible?[35]

These are the serious questions in life that we never take the time to answer. That may be a good thing, but it is thoughts like these that give you the inner smile you need to boost yourself out of a negative thought train. Whoo, Whoo!

David's 7 ½ Laws

Half Law: The following laws apply half the time
First Law: Things are usually easier than they look and if it turns out they're not, it's because there is a new lesson to learn that will save you down the road later.
Second Law: Things don't take as long as you would think they do. If they end up taking longer, it's

---

[35] With arthritis, even a sneeze can hurt; that's why when I'm not hurting, a sneeze is a celebration and I sneeze as loud as I can.

because you were going to have a fatal accident if the "thing" finished sooner.

Third Law: In any field of endeavor, anything that can go wrong probably won't, but if it does it's because you'll end up better off because it did.

Fourth Law: If there is a possibility that several things can go wrong, then the one that will cause the least damage will be the one to go wrong.

Fifth Law: If anything absolutely can NOT go wrong, it probably won't unless there is an advantage to it you don't know about yet.

Sixth Law: If you perceive that there are three possible solutions to a problem, but don't like any of them, then a fourth solution will promptly develop.

Seventh Law: Left to themselves, things tend to find their own resolutions; that is unless they are human.

Difference between highly humorous and lowly humorous:

An HHP will have every one laughing at a party with their astute observations on the funny quirks of the partygoers. The lowly humorous person will have everyone laughing by lighting their gas on fire and burning their ass. I don't know about you, but I'd rather have people enjoy my company without having to burn my ass in the process.

A Court Fable

Once upon a time there was a kingdom that had a king. The king's greatest wish was to rule the greatest kingdom in the world. He called all his advisors together to discuss what they would need to do to become the greatest kingdom in the world. "To be the greatest kingdom, we would need the greatest army," his general told him. "No, to be the greatest kingdom we would need the finest buildings and crafts for all to see," replied the king's chief architect. The court jester swayed into the room riding his unicycle. "Great and best are two different things. You may become one, but that does not necessarily make you the other. Which do you prefer?" The king thought a moment, "We should be the greatest and the best!" he replied. The king's chief advisor declared: "The king that listens to the fool, shall have a short rule." The jester finished the verse, "and the king who listens to his chief advisor will never become any wiser." The king smiled at his jester and asked, "What is the secret to becoming the greatest and the best?" The jester, still upon his unicycle said, "The key to becoming the greatest and the best is balance. Without balance you will fall." With that the jester dramatically fell off his unicycle and crashed into the chief advisor, knocking him over. "I'm so sorry chief." "You fool!" responded the chief advisor. "Yes, I am a fool, more than that I am a balanced fool. I spend time with my family, we go on wonderful grand vacations and mini-vacations throughout the year. I exercise regularly, I have a job that is fun and enjoyable," glancing at the king he added, "as long as I keep my head. When the kingdom strives for the balance that I have, it will become a better place to live and will have more than a good chance of becoming the greatest and best kingdom."

ENDING NUMBER ONE:

The king was pleased with his jester's remarks and made him his chief advisor. The jester became depressed in this position and eventually hung himself. The moral of the story is, if you have a good job that you like, don't just go for more money.

Or: Just because you have a balanced life doesn't mean everything is going to go your way. You do, however have a much better chance of living a joyful, enriching life.

ENDING NUMBER TWO:

The king was pleased with his jester's remarks and offered to make him his chief advisor. The jester respectfully declined saying it would throw his life out of balance and he would get too depressed in that position, which would not do him or the king any good. The king accepted this and went on to rule another twelve days. Then his chief advisor's plot to have him killed succeeded and civil war broke out in the kingdom, killing half the population. A foreign ruler took over who then helped it to become the greatest and best kingdom in the world.

A silly love poem (To nonsense)

My girl was mad, I couldn't love her
So I stuck my lip in a manhole cover

Because it hurt, she helped me out
My lip was swollen, I began to pout

She knew I was sad and she made me feel better
So I got her some pads to stick in her sweater

When she slapped me hard I understood
This gift I gave was not any good

She locked me up with an elephant full of gas

Luckily through the bars, I could pass

I tried to make up, by being funny
But instead she asked for all my money

Now we're both happy with what we've got
And decided it was time to tie the knot

I couldn't get a ring 'cause she had all my money
So her dad got it for me and called me "Sonny"

For years we think back to incidents with laughter
And we know we'll live happily ever after.

Here's to your living happily ever after and may you continue to expand your humor horizons.

David M. Jacobson
www.highlyhumorouspeople.com
dj@humorhorizons.com

The 7 ½ Habits of Highly Humorous People

Printed in the United States
83287LV00001B/1-267/A